PENGUIN ⊙ CLASSICS

THE PRINCE

NICCOLÒ MACHIAVELLI was born in Florence in 1469. He served the Florentine republic as a secretary and second chancellor, as ambassador and foreign policy-maker, but when the Medici family returned to power in 1512 he was suspected of conspiracy, imprisoned and tortured and forced to withdraw from public life. He retired to his farm near San Casciano, where he lived with his wife and six children and spent his time studying and writing. His most famous work, *The Prince*, was written in an attempt to gain favour with the Medicis and return to politics. Other works included the *Discourses on the First Decade of Livy*; *The Art of War*; and *Mandragola*, a satirical comedy. In 1520, Cardinal Giulio de' Medici secured him a commission to write a history of Florence, which he finished in 1525. Machiavelli died in 1527, after a brief return to public life.

TIM PARKS was born in Manchester in 1954 and moved to Italy in 1981, where he has lived ever since. He has written eleven novels including *Europa*, *Destiny*, *Cleaver* and, most recently, *Dreams of Rivers and Seas*, as well as a history of the Medici bank in fifteenth-century Florence, *Medici Money*. He lectures on literary translation in Milan and his many translations from the Italian include works by Moravia, Tabucchi, Calvino and Calasso.

NICCOLÒ MACHIAVELLI

The Prince

Translated and introduced by
TIM PARKS

PENGUIN BOOKS

PENGUIN BOOKS

Published by the Penguin Group
Penguin Books Ltd, 80 Strand, London WC2R ORL, England
Penguin Group (USA) Inc., 375 Hudson Street, New York, New York 10014, USA
Penguin Group (Canada), 90 Eglinton Avenue East, Suite 700, Toronto, Ontario, Canada M4P 2Y3
(a division of Pearson Penguin Canada Inc.)
Penguin Ireland, 25 St Stephen's Green, Dublin 2, Ireland (a division of Penguin Books Ltd)
Penguin Group (Australia), 250 Camberwell Road,
Camberwell, Victoria 3124, Australia (a division of Pearson Australia Group Pty Ltd)
Penguin Books India Pvt Ltd, 11 Community Centre, Panchsheel Park, New Delhi – 110 017, India
Penguin Group (NZ), 67 Apollo Drive, Rosedale, Auckland 0632, New Zealand
(a division of Pearson New Zealand Ltd)
Penguin Books (South Africa) (Pty) Ltd, 24 Sturdee Avenue, Rosebank,
Johannesburg 2196, South Africa

Penguin Books Ltd, Registered Offices: 80 Strand, London WC2R ORL, England

www.penguin.com

This translation first published 2009
This edition published 2011
006

Translation and editorial material © Tim Parks, 2009
All rights reserved

The moral right of the translator and editor has been asserted

Set in PostScript Adobe Sabon
Typeset by Ellipsis Books Limited, Glasgow
Printed in Great Britain by Clays Ltd, St Ives plc

Except in the United States of America, this book is sold subject
to the condition that it shall not, by way of trade or otherwise, be lent,
re-sold, hired out, or otherwise circulated without the publisher's
prior consent in any form of binding or cover other than that in
which it is published and without a similar condition including this
condition being imposed on the subsequent purchaser

ISBN: 978-0-141-44225-9

www.greenpenguin.co.uk

MIX
Paper from
responsible sources
FSC
www.fsc.org   FSC™ C018179

Penguin Books is committed to a sustainable
future for our business, our readers and our planet.
This book is made from Forest Stewardship
Council™ certified paper.

Contents

THE PRINCE

Introduction

Necessity. Must. Have to. Inevitably. Bound to. These are the words that recur insistently throughout *The Prince*. And then again: *success, victory, prestige, achievement,* and, on the other hand: *loss, failure, defeat, death.* These opposites are linked together by an almost obsessive use of *because, so that, hence, therefore, as a result, as a consequence.* From start to finish we have a vision of man manoeuvring precariously in a suffocating net of cause and effect. What is at stake is survival. Anything extra is luxury.

The Prince was written by a forty-four-year-old diplomat facing ruin. After fourteen years of influence and prestige, a change of regime had led to his dismissal. Suspected of conspiring against the new government, he was imprisoned and tortured. The rapid reversal of fortunes could not have been more devastating. Found innocent and released, he left town to live with his wife and family on a small farm. For a worldly man and compulsive womanizer, used to being at the frenetic heart of public life, this too felt like punishment. Idle and bitter, he tramped the hills by day and, in the long, empty evenings, began to write down some considerations on how to win power and, above all, how to hold on to it, how *not* to be a victim of circumstance. The result was a slim volume that would be a scandal for centuries.

Niccolò Machiavelli was born in Florence in 1469, the same year Lorenzo de' Medici (il Magnifico) came to power.

First male child after two daughters, Niccolò would grow up very close to his father, Bernardo, an ex-lawyer, mostly unemployed, with good contacts but no significant wealth or influence. If the son was to rise in the world, and he was determined to do so, he would have to count on his own wits and charm. Niccolò's younger brother, Totto, chose not to compete and went into the priesthood. The boys' mother, it should be said, was an extremely devout woman, a writer of religious poems and hymns. Their father on the other hand was sceptical, more at home with the sober works of Latin antiquity than the Bible. Niccolò may have taken his writing skills from his mother, but over divisions on religion he stood with his father and the Roman historians.

One says of Lorenzo il Magnifico that he 'came to power', but officially Florence was a republic and since Lorenzo was only twenty years old in 1469 he was far too young to hold elected office; an explanation is required. When, in the thirteenth century, the Florentines had thrown out the noble families who used to run the town, they introduced a republican constitution of exemplary idealism. A government of eight *priori* led by one *gonfaloniere*, or prime minister, would be elected every two months by drawing tags from a series of bags containing the names of well-to-do men from different guilds and different areas of town. This lottery would allow each major profession and each geographical area to be adequately and constantly represented. Every individual (of a certain social standing) could expect a brief share of power in order that no one could ever seize it permanently.

The system was unworkable. Every two months a new government might take a different position on key issues. The potential for instability more or less obliged whichever family was in the ascendant to step in and impose continuity. From 1434 on, the Medicis – first Cosimo, then Piero, then Lorenzo – had been manipulating the electoral process to make sure that most of the names in the bags were friendly to themselves and that all of those actually selected for government would toe the Medici line. Hence, although the Florentines still liked to boast that they were free citizens who bowed the knee to no man, by the mid-fifteenth century they were in fact living in something very close to a dictatorship. When the rival Pazzi family tried to assassinate Lorenzo in the Duomo in April 1478, it was because they saw no legitimate way of putting him in his place as an ordinary citizen. Machiavelli thus grew up in a society where the distance between how things were actually run and how they were described as being run could not have been greater. He was close to his ninth birthday when the captured Pazzi conspirators, one an archbishop, were hung upside down from the high windows of the city's main government building and left there for weeks to rot. He would have understood very young the price of getting it wrong in politics.

The young Machiavelli might also have had reason to doubt that there was any meaningful difference between matters of religion and matters of state. The pope had backed the Pazzi conspiracy, priests had been involved in the assassination attempt and Lorenzo was excommunicated after it failed; the religious edict was a political tool. A war between Florence and Rome ensued and the hostility only ended in 1480 when Turkish raids on the southern Italian coast prompted a rare moment of unity in the peninsula. Years later, Lorenzo would so ingratiate himself with a new pope as to get his son Giovanni made a cardinal at age thirteen. From excommunication to pope's favourite was quite a change of fortune and once again it was more a matter of politics than of faith. Nothing, it appeared, was beyond the reach of wealth and astute negotiation.

At this point Machiavelli was twenty-one. We know very little of his early adult life, but one thing he definitely did at least once was to listen to the fiery preacher Girolamo Savonarola, head of the influential monastery of San Marco.

Savonarola's was a different kind of Christianity: rather than the corrupt, pleasure-conscious world of the papacy, whose decadence had offered no resistance to the rise of Humanism, this austere monk represented an early manifestation of what we have come to call fundamentalism, a return to the biblical text as the sole authority on earth and a vision of the Church as embattled and defensive in a world increasingly interested in values that had little to do with the gospel story. With great conviction, Savonarola preached the virtues of poverty, advocated the burning of any book or work of art that was impure and prophesied doom for the sinful Florentines in the form of a foreign invasion. In 1494 his prophesy came true.

To get any grasp of Machiavelli's diplomatic career and the range of reference he draws on in *The Prince*, one must have some sense of the complicated political geography of Italy in the fifteenth and early sixteenth centuries, and of the profound change that occurred in the 1490s, a change that would determine Italy's fate for the next 350 years.

For most of the fifteenth century there had been five major players in the peninsula: the Kingdom of Naples, the Papal States, Florence, Venice and Milan. Extending from just south of Rome to the southernmost tip of Calabria, the Kingdom of Naples was by far the largest. Wedged in the centre, with only precarious access to the sea, Florence was the smallest and weakest.

All five powers were in fierce competition for whatever territory they could take. Having lost much of their overseas empire to the Turks, the Venetians were eager to expand inside the northern Italian plain (Ferrara, Verona, Brescia) and down the Adriatic coast (Forlì, Rimini). Conscious of the size and power of a now unified France to the north, Milan hoped for gains to the south and west (Genoa) as a counterweight. Florence simply tried to get bigger in any way that was convenient. Over the previous century the Florentines had captured Arezzo, Pisa and Cortona and wasted huge energies in a series of failed attempts to conquer Lucca.

Rome's aim under any pope was always to expand north and east into Romagna and Emilia, with a view to swallowing up Perugia, Bologna, Rimini and Forlì, a project that would bring it into conflict with both Venice and Florence. In the far south, Naples was governed by a branch of the house of Aragon, but the crown was contested by the Angevin kings of France and by the Spanish royal family (also Aragons) which already ruled Sicily.

So the scenario was complicated. Scattered between the large states were at least a score of smaller ones, some no bigger than a town and the surrounding fields, and all constantly under threat of invasion from one enemy or another. However, if the situation was rarely static, it is also true that there were few major changes. As soon as one power achieved some significant military victory, the others immediately formed an alliance against it to halt its progress. Florence, in particular, owed its continuing independence largely to the fact that if Venice, Milan or Rome tried to take it, the other two would at once intervene to prevent this happening. So for more than a hundred years a certain balance of power had been kept. All this ended with the French invasion of 1494.

The invasion was, as Machiavelli himself explains in *The Prince*, largely the Italians' own fault. For some time the five states had been in the habit of frightening each other with the threat of foreign intervention. During the war against Rome and Naples in 1480, Florence had invited the French king to pursue his claim to the throne of Naples more actively. In 1482, during a Venetian assault on Ferrara, Florence and Milan had encouraged the Turks to step up their attacks on Venice's maritime possessions. Venice had replied by inviting the Duke of Orleans to pursue his claim to Milan. In a war against Naples in 1483, Pope Innocent VIII had reminded the

Duke of Lorraine that he too had a claim to the southern kingdom and invited him to send troops.

There was an element of bluff and brinkmanship in these threats, but in 1494 when King Charles VIII of France accepted Milan's invitation to make good his claim to the crown of Naples, the bluff was called. Charles marched south with an army far larger than any Italians had seen in living memory. From that moment on, the peninsula would not be free from foreign intervention until the completion of the Risorgimento in 1870. Struggling to hold Naples, the French would invite in the Spanish from Sicily to split the kingdom with them, and the Spanish, after Charles I of Spain inherited the crown of the Holy Roman Empire, would eventually push France back north of the Alps, put Rome to the sack and dominate Italy for 150 years.

But that is to leap ahead. In 1494, when the French first marched through Lombardy heading for Naples, Florence was directly in their path and, what's more, an ally of Naples. At this point Lorenzo il Magnifico had been dead for two years and the Medici regime was led by his incompetent son, Piero. So abject was Piero's capitulation to Charles, so spineless his decision simply to surrender the city's dependent territories, that the Florentines rebelled against him. The Medici regime collapsed and very soon the preacher who had been prophesying this disaster was made *gonfaloniere*, first minister, this time on a yearly, rather than a two-monthly, basis.

Girolamo Savonarola ruled Florence from 1494 to 1498, during which time the city passed from being one of the centres of Renaissance Humanism to a book-burning, fundamentalist theocracy. Realizing that Savonarola's claim to be God's prophet was a far greater threat to its authority than any Humanism, scepticism or eclecticism, the Church in Rome did everything possible to bring about his downfall and in 1498, having lost much of his support in Florence, the preacher was convicted of heresy and burned at the stake. It was shortly after these dramatic events that Niccolò Machiavelli succeeded in getting himself elected to the important positions of Secretary of the Second Chancery (one of two key state departments in Florence) and, soon afterwards, Secretary of the Ten of War, a committee that dealt with foreign relations and war preparations.

Machiavelli was twenty-eight. We have no idea how he arrived at such appointments at this early age. There is no record of any special experience that would warrant such confidence in his abilities. But within months he was travelling to neighbouring states to represent Florence's interests, and over the next fourteen years he would be involved in important, often long-drawn-out missions to the King of France, the pope, the Holy Roman Emperor, Cesare Borgia, Caterina Sforza and many others. In between these missions he was frequently and very actively engaged in Florence's ongoing military campaign to re-take Pisa, which had regained its independence during the French invasion. Pisa was crucial to Florentine commerce in that it gave the town an outlet to the sea.

Introductions to *The Prince* generally play down Machiavelli's abilities as a diplomat, presenting these years as useful only in so far as they offered him the material he would draw on for his writing after he had lost his position. Machiavelli would not have seen things that way. For more than a decade he was Florence's top diplomat and proud to be so, and if the missions he undertook did not produce spectacular results this was largely because he was representing the weakest of the main states in Italy in a period of particular confusion and vulnerability that would eventually see four foreign powers militarily involved in the peninsula: France, Spain, the Holy Roman Empire and Switzerland.

Savonarola had taken Florence towards an alliance with France; the priest's successors followed the same policy, but without any clear vision of how the city might achieve stability and security in the long term. To make matters worse, having decided in 1502 that their *gonfaloniere*, or first minister, should be elected for life, the Florentines gave the job to Piero Soderini, an honourable man but chronically incapable of making any kind of bold decision. Machiavelli's diplomatic career was thus mostly taken up in attempts to persuade surrounding and threatening states to leave Florence alone and not to expect financial or military help from her for their wars elsewhere; that is, as far as there was a discernible, long-term policy it was one of prevarication. Far from home, Machiavelli would frequently receive contradictory orders after he had already started negotiating. Arriving in foreign towns, he would find that his expense allowance wasn't sufficient to pay couriers to take his messages back to Florence. Sometimes he could barely afford to feed and clothe himself. Such was the contempt of the more powerful monarchs that he was often obliged to wait days or even weeks before being granted an audience.

It is in the light of these frustrations that we have to understand Machiavelli's growing obsession, very much in evidence in *The Prince*, with the formation of a citizen army. Florence was weak partly because of its size but mostly because it had no military forces of its own. It relied on mercenary armies which were notorious for evaporating when things got tough, before the gates of Pisa for example. A power-base built on an efficient and patriotic civilian army would give a diplomat like Machiavelli a little more clout and respect when he negotiated. Or so he hoped.

In June of 1502, four years into the job, Machiavelli met Cesare Borgia, son of Pope Alexander VI. With his father's support, Borgia was carving out a new state for himself on the northern borders of the Papal States and had just captured the city of Urbino to the east of Florence. Sent on a mission to dissuade Borgia from advancing into Florentine territory, Machiavelli was deeply impressed by the man. Seductive, determined, cunning and ruthless, Borgia was a leader in the epic mode. Certainly he could hardly have been more different from the diplomat's dithering boss, Soderini.

Machiavelli was on another mission to Borgia in January 1503 when the adventurer invited a group of rebels to negotiations in the coastal town of Senigallia, then had them seized and murdered as soon as they were inside the town walls. Here was a man, Machiavelli realized, determined to take circumstance by the scruff of the neck. It was not so much Borgia's willingness to ignore Christian principles that fascinated him, as his ability to assess a situation rapidly, make his calculations, then act decisively in whatever way would bring the desired result. This modern, positivist attitude, where thought and analysis serve in so far as they produce decisive action, rather than abstract concepts, lies at the heart of *The Prince*.

Meanwhile Florence continued to drift. Machiavelli was once again on the scene in 1503, this time in Rome, when Borgia's empire collapsed after both he and his father fell seriously ill; legend has it that Alexander had accidentally poisoned them both. The pope died and the son lost his power-base. Three years later Machiavelli was travelling with the later Pope Julius at the head of the papal army when Julius demanded admission to the town of Perugia, walked in with only a small bodyguard and told the local tyrant, Giampaolo Baglioni, to get out or face certain defeat. Sure that Baglioni would simply kill Julius, Machiavelli was amazed when the man caved in and fled. Such were the pope's coercive powers as he then marched north to lay siege to Bologna that Florence was once again forced to enter an alliance and a war in which it had no desire to be involved.

As Secretary of the Ten of War, Machiavelli enjoyed just one moment of personal glory, in 1509, when the citizen army that he had finally been allowed to form overcame Pisan resistance and took the town after a long siege. Given the many failed attempts to capture Pisa using mercenary armies, this victory was a powerful vindication of Machiavelli's conviction that citizen armies were superior. It was also the only occasion in his fourteen years of service when Soderini took the initiative with success.

But in every other respect things went from bad to worse. Florence was living on borrowed time, its freedom dependent on the whims of others. Three years after the capture of Pisa, when Pope Julius, now in alliance with the Spanish, defeated the French at Ravenna, he immediately sent an army to Florence to impose a return of the Medici and transform the city into a puppet state dependent on Rome. After brief resistance, the Florentine army was crushed at Prato a few miles to the north of the city. Soderini escaped and the Medici returned. Machiavelli was unemployed and unemployable.

The scandalous nature of *The Prince* was largely determined by its structure rather than any conscious desire to shock. Originally entitled *On Principalities*, the book opens with an attempt to categorize different kinds of states and governments at different moments of their development, then, moving back and forth between ancient and modern history, to establish some universal principles relative to the business of taking and holding power in each kind of state. Given Machiavelli's experience, wide reading and determined intellectual honesty, the project obliged him to explain that there were many occasions when winning and holding political power was possible only if a leader was ready to act outside the moral codes that applied to ordinary individuals. Public opinion was such, he explained, that, once victory was achieved, nobody was going to put the winner on trial. Political leaders were above the law.

Had Machiavelli insisted on deploring this unhappy state of affairs, had he dwelt on other criteria for judging a leader, aside from his mere ability to stay in power and build a strong state, had he told us with appropriate piety that power was hardly worth having if you had to sell your soul to get it, he could have headed off a great deal of criticism while still delivering the same information. But aside from one or two token regrets that the world is not a nicer place, Machiavelli does not do this. It wasn't his project. Rather he takes it for granted that we already know that life, particularly political life, is routinely, and sometimes unspeakably, cruel, and that once established in a position of power a ruler may have no choice but to kill or be killed.

This is where the words 'of necessity', 'must' and 'have to' become so ominous. For *The Prince* is most convincing and most scandalous not in its famous general statements – that the end justifies the means, that men must be pampered or crushed, that the only sure way of keeping a conquered territory is to devastate it utterly, and so on – but in the many historical examples of barbarous behaviour that Machiavelli puts before us, without any hand-wringing, as things that were *bound to happen*: the Venetians find that their mercenary leader Carmagnola is not putting much effort into his fighting any more, but they are afraid that if they dismiss him he will walk off with the territory he previously captured for them: 'at which point the only safe thing to do was to kill him.' Hiero of Syracuse, when given command of his country's army, finds that they are all mercenaries and 'realizing that they could neither make use of them, nor let them go, he had them all cut to pieces.'

The climax of this approach comes with Machiavelli's presentation of the ruthless Cesare Borgia as a model for any man determined to win a state for himself (as if such a project were not essentially dissimilar from building a house or starting a business). Having tamed and unified the Romagna with the help of his cruel minister Remirro de Orco, Machiavelli tells us, Borgia decided to deflect people's hatred away from himself by putting the blame for all atrocities on his minister and then doing away with him: so 'he had de Orco beheaded and his corpse put on display one morning in the piazza in Cesena with a wooden block and a bloody knife beside. The ferocity of the spectacle left people both gratified and shocked.'

It's hard not to feel, as we read the chapters on Borgia, that this is the point where Machiavelli's book ceases to be the learned, but fairly tame, *On Principalities* and is transformed into the extraordinary and disturbing work that would eventually be called *The Prince*. In short, Machiavelli's attention has shifted from a methodical analysis of different political systems to a gripping and personally engaged account of the psychology of the leader who has placed himself beyond the constrictions of Christian ethics and lives in a delirium of pure power. For a diplomat like Machiavelli, who had spent his life among the powerful but never really held the knife by the handle, a state employee so scrupulously honest that when investigated for embezzlement he ended up being reimbursed monies that were due to him, it was all too easy to fall into a state of envy and almost longing when contemplating the awesome Borgia who had no qualms about taking anything that came his way and never dreamed of being honest to anyone.

At a deep level, then, the scandal of *The Prince* is intimately tied up with the scandal of all writers of fiction and history who in the quiet of their studies take vicarious enjoyment in the ruthlessness of the characters they describe – but with this difference: Machiavelli systematizes such behaviour and appears to recommend it, if only to those few who are committed to winning and holding political power. The author's description, in a letter to a friend, of his state of mind when writing the book makes it clear what a relief it was, during these months immediately following his dismissal, imprisonment and torture, to imagine himself back in the world of politics and, if only on paper, on a par with history's great heroes.

Come evening, I walk home and go into my study. In the
passage I take off my ordinary clothes, caked with mud and
slime, and put on my formal palace gowns. Then when I'm
properly dressed I take my place in the courts of the past where
the ancients welcome me kindly and I eat my fill of the *only*
food that is really mine and that I was born for. I'm quite at
ease talking to them and asking them why they did the things
they did, and they are generous with their answers. So for four
hours at a time I feel no pain, I forget all my worries, I'm not
afraid of poverty and death doesn't frighten me. I put myself
entirely in their minds.

In so far as *The Prince* remains a persuasive account of
how political power is won and lost it is so because it eventually focuses on the mind, or, to be more precise, on the
interaction of individual and collective psychologies, the latter
fairly predictable, the former infinitely varied, the two together dangerously volatile. The book is not a careful elab-
oration of a rigid, predetermined vision. More and more,
as Machiavelli rapidly assesses different kinds of states and
forms of government, different contexts, different men and
their successes and failures, he runs up against two factors
that defy codification: the role of luck and the mystery of
personality. By the end of the book he is beyond the stage of
offering heroes and success stories as models, aware that if
there is one circumstance that a man cannot easily change it
is his own character: even had he wanted to, Soderini could
not have modelled himself on Borgia, nor vice versa.

In particular Machiavelli is fascinated by the way certain
personality traits can mesh positively or negatively with certain sets of historical circumstances. A man can be successful
in one situation then fail miserably in another; a policy that
works well in one moment is a disaster the next. Rather than
one ideal ruler, then, different men are required for different
situations. The only key to permanent political success would

be always to adapt one's deepest instincts to new events, but, as Machiavelli ruefully observes, that would effectively mean the end of 'luck' and the end of history.

Machiavelli's own mind was deeply divided during the writing of *The Prince* and it is the resulting tension that accounts for much of the book's fascination and ambiguity. On the one hand, as a form of private therapy, he was disinterestedly pursuing the truth about power and politics: to establish how states really were won and lost would give him an illusion of control and bolster his self-esteem. At the same time, and perhaps less consciously, he was vicariously enjoying, in the stories of Borgia and others, the sort of dramatic political achievements that had always been denied to him. In this regard it's interesting to see how rapidly he glosses over Borgia's abject fall from power, his arrest, imprisonment and death, almost as if the author were in denial about his hero's ultimate fallibility.

Therapeutic as this might have been, however, at another level *The Prince* was clearly written for publication and meant as a public performance. Machiavelli loves to show off his intelligence, his range of reference, his clever reasoning. Even here, though, his intentions were divided and perhaps contradictory. At his most passionate and focused he was involved in a debate with all the great historians and philosophers of the past and determined to show his contemporaries that his own mind was as sharp as the best. But in a more practical mood Machiavelli was planning to use the book as a passport to get himself back into a job: so evident and compelling, he hoped, would his analytical skills appear, that the ruler to whom he formally gave and dedicated the book would necessarily want to employ him; hence the flattering tone of the opening dedication and the addition of *The Prince*'s final patriotic pages proposing that the ruler in question should be the man to rid Italy of foreign oppression.

Who was this ruler? Shortly before Machiavelli had been

released from prison, Pope Julius had died and been replaced by Giovanni de' Medici, il Magnifico's son, the man
who had become a cardinal at thirteen. This was March 1513.
When he started work on *The Prince* some months later,
Machiavelli had intended to dedicate the book to Giovanni's
brother, Giuliano, who had been put in charge of Florence
after the Medicis' return. However, when the effeminate
Giuliano began to move away from politics and was replaced
in Florence by his aggressive, warlike nephew Lorenzo,
Machiavelli decided to switch the dedication to the younger
man.

Thus far the writer showed himself flexible in the face of
changing events. Yet there is something ingenuous and almost
endearing in the clever diplomat's miscalculation here. The
brilliant reasoning required to convince yourself that you had
got a grip on politics and history, the profound analysis that
would demonstrate to your fellow intellectuals that you were
as clear-headed as Livy, Tacitus and Thucydides put together,
were not the qualities that a young and hardly well-read
Medici prince was likely to comprehend, never mind enjoy.

Given the book in 1515, Lorenzo probably never opened
it and certainly didn't take time to study Machiavelli's carefully crafted reflections. Then, even if he had read it, would
Lorenzo, or indeed any other ruler, have wanted to employ a
diplomat who had gone on record as saying that trickery
was largely the name of the game and that though it wasn't
important to have a religious faith it was absolutely essential
to *appear* to have one? Machiavelli should have been the
first to understand that as an instrument for furthering his
diplomatic career, rather than a literary and philosophical
achievement in its own right, the book's honesty would be
self-defeating: the two goals were never compatible.

Surprised and disappointed by *The Prince*'s failure, Machiavelli went back to womanizing. Aside from routine whoring,
he fell in and out of love easily, pursuing passion without

discretion or restraint. And just as he had more luck with romance than diplomacy, he had more success when he wrote ironic, sex-centred comedies rather than candid but dangerous political analyses. In 1518 the first performance of his play *The Mandragola*, in which a young man invents the most absurd subterfuges to get a married woman into bed, won Machiavelli immediate celebrity; some years later *Clizia*, which this time has an older man hell-bent on having his way with a very young woman, confirmed his talent.

But literary success was not enough for Machiavelli. It was active politics that interested him, and, though he laboured for ten years or so on his *Discourses on Livy*, then on a long history of Florence and finally on a short work entitled *The Art of War*, it was his old job as the city's principal ambassador that he always yearned for. Finally, in 1525, Pope Clement VII, alias Giulio de' Medici (Giovanni's cousin), drew the ex-diplomat back into politics, asking him for advice on how to deal with the growing antagonism between the French and the Spanish. As an eventual clash between the two great powers inside Italy loomed ever closer, Machiavelli was given the task of overseeing Florence's defensive walls. When the crunch came, however, and the armies of Spain and the Holy Roman Empire, now united under the same crown, marched south into Italy, they simply bypassed Florence, went straight to Rome and sacked it. It was an occasion of the most disgraceful savagery on a scale Italy had not witnessed for centuries. In the aftermath, the Medici regime in Florence collapsed and once again Machiavelli was out of favour. Overwhelmed with disappointment and in the habit of taking medicines that weren't good for him, he died in June 1527, aged fifty-eight, having accepted, no doubt after careful calculation, extreme unction.

That there are many different roads to notoriety and that a man's achievements may combine with historical events in unexpected ways, are truths Machiavelli was well aware of. So he would have appreciated the irony that it was largely due to Luther's Protestant reform and the ensuing wars of religion that his name became the object of the most implacable vilification and, as a consequence, universally famous.

The turning point came in 1572. *The Prince* had not been published in Machiavelli's lifetime. After circulating for years in manuscript form, then in a printed Latin edition (still entitled *On Principalities*), it finally appeared in Italian in 1532, only to be put on Pope Paul IV's Index of Prohibited Books in 1559, this partly in response to the prompting of the English cardinal Reginald Pole, who maintained that, written as it was by 'Satan's finger', *The Prince* was largely responsible for Henry VIII's decision to take the English Church away from Rome.

Meantime, in France, the conflict between the Protestant Huguenots and the Catholics was intensifying and would reach a head under the reign of the sickly young Charles IX, who for the most part was controlled by his mother, the Italian, indeed Florentine, Catherine de' Medici, daughter of the same Lorenzo de' Medici to whom Machiavelli had dedicated *The Prince*. Catherine had brought a great many Italian favourites into the French court, a move guaranteed to arouse anti-Italian feeling. In general, she sought to dampen down the religious conflict which threatened to tear France apart, but nevertheless she would be held responsible for the St Bartholomew's Day Massacre of 1572 when thousands of Huguenots were murdered. One potential victim, Innocent Gentillet, escaped to Protestant Geneva and wrote a *Discours contre Machiavel* that was to set the tone for anti-Machiavellian criticism for decades to come.

Intended as an attack on Catherine de' Medici and militant French Catholicism, and hence a defence of the Huguenots, the book described Catherine as a compulsive reader of Machiavelli and, playing on anti-Italian feeling, claimed that both queen and writer were representative of a callous and villainous trait in Italian national character. Listed out of context, the ideas developed in *The Prince* were schematized and simplified, allowing readers to imagine they had read Machiavelli himself when what they were actually getting was a travesty that legitimized any form of brutality and rejoiced in amoral calculation.

From this point on, Machiavelli's name escaped from the restricted circle of intellectual reflection and became a popular term of denigration. 'Mach Evil' and 'Match-a-villain' were typical English corruptions, 'Mitchell Wylie' a Scottish. Many critics would not bother reading his work in the original but take their information from Gentillet, whose 'Anti-Machiavel', as his book became known, was quickly translated into Latin for English readers and then, some twenty years later, directly into English. At this point (the end of the sixteenth century) the first English translation of Machiavelli's work was yet to appear.

Ironically, in the years after the St Bartholomew's Day Massacre, as Catherine de' Medici struggled to find some solution to France's civil wars, and in particular to convince Catholics of the need to tolerate the existence of the Huguenots, if only in Huguenot enclaves, both she and her supposed mentor Machiavelli once again came under attack, this time from the Catholic side. The accusation now was that, in the attempt to avoid conflict, religious truths of supreme importance were being subordinated to questions of political convenience, something that would eventually transform France, the Catholics feared, into a secular state.

Here the criticism comes closer to the real spirit of Machiavelli. Renaissance Humanism in general had shifted the focus of intellectual reflection from questions of theology and metaphysical truth to matters of immediate and practical human interest. In general, however, lip service had always been paid to the ultimate superiority of religious matters and writers had avoided suggesting that there might be a profound incompatibility between rival value systems: it was perfectly possible, that is, to be a good Christian and an effective political leader.

Machiavelli, on the contrary, made it clear that, as he saw it, Christian principles and effective political leadership were not always compatible; situations would arise where one was bound to choose between the two. It was not, as his critics claimed, that he rejected all ethical values outright; the strength, unity and independence of a people and state certainly constituted goals worth fighting for ('I love my country more than my soul', Machiavelli declared in a letter to fellow historian Francesco Guicciardini). But such goals could not always be achieved without abandoning Christian principles; two value-systems were at loggerheads. To make matters worse, Machiavelli did not appear to be concerned about this. He took it as an evident truth: Christian principles were admirable, but not applicable for politicians in certain circumstances; the idea that all human behaviour could be assessed in relation to one set of values was naive and utopian. It was in so far as Machiavelli allowed these dangerous implications to surface in his writing that he both unmasked, and himself became identified with, what we might call the unacceptable face of Renaissance Humanism.

How much the presentation of the Machiavellian villain in Elizabethan and Jacobean drama, from Kyd and Marlowe, through to Middleton, Shakespeare and ultimately Ben Jonson, owed to Gentillet's 'Anti-Machiavel' and how much to a direct knowledge of Machiavelli's writings is still a matter of academic dispute. In the 1580s an Italian version of *The Prince* was printed in England, avoiding a publication ban by claiming falsely on the frontispiece that it was printed in Italy. Many educated English people at the time had a good knowledge of Italian. Sir Francis Bacon had certainly read *The Prince* before its first legal publication in English in 1640, defending the Florentine in the *Advancement of Learning* (1605) with the remark: 'We are much beholden to Machiavel and others, that write what men do and not what they ought to do.'

But the 'murderous Machiavel' who gets more than 400 mentions in Elizabethan drama, thus making the Florentine's name synonymous with the idea of villainy for centuries to come, is another matter. The Roman author Seneca had long ago established a tradition in tragic drama that featured an evil, calculating tyrant who would stop at nothing to grasp all the power he could. Renaissance Italian theatre had updated this type of villain with elements from Machiavelli, transforming the character into an unscrupulous courtier who takes pleasure in wicked calculation and cruelty. It was from this model that the English theatre developed its endless manifestations of the devious rogue (pander, miser, or revengeful cuckold) who administers poisons with aplomb and is never without a dagger beneath his cloak.

From the point of view of the dramatist, an unscrupulous character who has a secret agenda and relies on his presumed intellectual superiority to dupe those around him is obviously an exciting proposition. Such a figure can be depended upon to create tension, keep the plot moving and allow for resolutions where the larger group's benign order once again imposes itself after the tragic disturbance caused by the wicked, scheming individual. Beyond a superficial repulsion that the audience feels towards such a character, be it Marlowe's Jew of Malta, Webster's Flamineo in *The White Devil*, or Shakespeare's Iago, there is also an undercurrent of excitement at the thought that it might be possible to take life entirely into one's hands, manipulate people and circumstances at will and generally pursue one's selfish goals without a thought for moral codes or eternal damnation: in this sense the Machiavellian villain looks ahead to the worst of modern individualism.

Then there was also, of course, the contrasting pleasure of seeing the clever schemer 'hoist with his own petard'. As the years passed and the high tension of Jacobean tragedy relaxed into the comedies of Ben Jonson and his contemporaries, the evil Machiavel became a pathetic failure whose complacently wicked designs inevitably and reassuringly led to his making a fool of himself. Fading out of British drama in the mid-seventeenth century, this stock figure is still resurrected from time to time, most recently and hilariously in Rowan Atkinson's Blackadder, a character who adds a visceral cowardice to the already long list of Machiavel's vices.

To a great extent, no doubt, it was this identification of Machiavelli's name with everything that was evil which kept *The Prince* in print and guaranteed that, despite the papal ban, it would be widely read. But there was more. As medieval Christianity and scholasticism sank into the past and science and reason made their slow, often unwelcome advances, as Europe got used to religious schism and competing versions of the truth, the overriding question for any modern ruler inevitably became: how can I convince people that I have a legitimate, *reasonable* right to hold power and to govern? In England Charles Stuart would insist on the notion that kings had a divine right, this at a time when so many English monarchs had seized their crowns by force and cunning. Curiously enough, Charles's great antagonist Cromwell felt that he too had a direct line to God and legitimacy, but through belief and piety rather than family and inheritance. Officially a parliamentarian, Cromwell frequently governed without parliament or elections for fear the people might not see things God's way.

Meantime, across Europe, the princes and princesses of ancient noble families took to marrying and remarrying each other in an ever-thickening web of defensive alliances, as if density of blood and lineage might offer protection against the threat of usurpers or, worse still, republicanism and democracy. No family was more practised at this up-market dating game than the Medici, who, partly thanks to an extraordinary network of connections, would hang on in Florence in a client-state twilight lasting more than 200 undistinguished years. Meantime, from Paris to Madrid to Naples, the court clothes became finer, the statues and monuments more pompous and the whole royal charade more colourful and more solemn, as though people might somehow be dazzled into believing that a king or a duke really did have a right to rule. Many prestigious works of art were commissioned with precisely this idea in mind.

But most of all Europe's rulers worked hard to put a halo round their crowned heads, to appear religious and at all costs to uphold the Faith, sensing that this too would bolster their position and draw attention away from the mystery of their privileges. Later still, particularly after the French Revolution had destroyed any illusions about the rights of monarchs, the rather desperate card of 'respectability' was played. Members of court, Napoleon ordered, shortly after usurping power, must attend soirées *with their wives*, to appear respectable and avoid gossip. 'The death of conversation', Talleyrand opined. Certainly, when a leader has to rely on appearing *respectable* to claim legitimacy, he is on thin ice indeed.

To this long-drawn-out conspiracy of pomp and pious circumstance, Machiavelli's little book was a constant threat. It reminded people that power is always up for grabs, always a question of what can be taken by force or treachery, and always, despite all protests to the contrary, the prime concern of any ruler. In their attempt to discredit *The Prince*, both religious and state authorities played up the author's admiration for the ruthless Borgia, and never mentioned his perception that in the long run a ruler must avoid being hated by his people and must always put their interests before those of the aristocracy; the people are so many, Machiavelli reflected, that power ultimately lies with them.

Liberal and left-wing thinkers were not slow to pick up on this aspect of the book. As Rousseau saw it, the whole of *The Prince* was itself a Machiavellian ruse: the author had only pretended to give lessons to kings whereas in fact his real aim was to teach people to be free by showing them that royal power was no more than subterfuge. Both Spinoza and, later, the Italian poet Ugo Foscolo saw it the same way: *The Prince* was a cautionary tale about how power really worked, the underlying intention being to deprive those who held it of dignity and glamour and teach the people as a whole how to resist it; Machiavelli after all declared himself a republican and a libertarian. The communist leader Antonio Gramsci would even see *The Prince* as looking forward to the dictatorship of the proletariat.

Others took a more traditional view: Bertrand Russell described *The Prince* as 'a handbook for gangsters', and in so doing did no more than repeat the position of Frederick the Great, who wrote a book to refute Machiavelli and present a more idealistic vision of monarchical government. Others again (Jakob Burckhardt and Friedrich Meinecke) found a space between denigration and admiration to suggest that the novelty of Machiavelli was to present leadership and nation-building as creative processes that should be judged not morally but *aesthetically*; in a manner that looked forward to Nietzsche the charismatic leader made a work of art of himself and his government. Mussolini simply took the book at face value: it was a useful '*vade mecum* for statesmen', he enthused.

But whatever our interpretation of his intentions, one reaction that Machiavelli never seems to provoke is indifference. Reading *The Prince* it is impossible not to engage with the disturbing notion that politics cannot be governed by the ethical codes that most of us seek to observe in our ordinary lives. And however we react to this idea, once we have closed the book it will be very hard to go on thinking of our own leaders in quite the same way as we did before.

Translator's Note

Translations have a way of gathering dust. This isn't true of an original text. When we read Chaucer or Shakespeare we may need a gloss, or in the case of Chaucer a modern translation, but we only look at these things so that we can then enjoy the work as it was first written. And we're struck by its immediacy and freshness, as if we had been able to learn a foreign language in a very short space of time with little effort and maximum reward.

This is not the case with an old translation. If we read Pope's translation of Homer today, we read it because we want to read Pope, not Homer. Linguistically, the translation draws our attention more to the language and poetry of our eighteenth century than to Homer or ancient Greece.

So to attempt a new translation of Machiavelli is not to dismiss previous translations as poor. We are just acknowledging that these older versions now draw attention to themselves as moments in the English language. My efforts of course will some day meet the same fate. Such distractions are particularly unfortunate with Machiavelli, who insisted that he was only interested in style in so far as it could deliver content without frills or distraction. 'I haven't prettified the book,' he tells us, 'or padded it out with long sentences or pompous, pretentious words, or any of the irrelevant flourishes and attractions so many writers use; I didn't want it to please for anything but the range and seriousness of its subject matter.'

I have taken that statement of intention as my guide in this translation, attempting wherever possible to free the text from the archaisms and corrosive quaintness of older English versions, to get to the essential meaning of the original and deliver it, as we say today, but perhaps not tomorrow, straight.

It isn't easy. The first problem, and one that sets up all the others, is already there in the title: *The Prince*. What is a prince for Machiavelli? Well, a duke is a prince. The pope is a prince. A Roman emperor is a prince. The King of France is a prince. The Lord of Imola is a prince.

This won't work in modern English. The English have Prince Charles. And the thing about Prince Charles is that he is not King Charles and probably never will be. And even if he were king he would wield no real power, not even the kind of power the pope wields, and we never think of the pope as a king or prince.

The only other idea we have of 'the prince', in English, is Prince Charming. This concept is a long way from the ageing Prince Charles and even further from the kind of prince Machiavelli was talking about. Machiavelli's word 'prince' does not mean 'the son of the king', and even less 'an attractive young suitor'. Machiavelli's *'principe'* refers generically to men of power, men who rule a state. The prince is the first, or principal, man.

So the translator is tempted to use the word 'king'. At least in the past a king stood at the apex of a hierarchical system, he was the man who mattered. But it is difficult, translating Machiavelli, to use the word 'king' to refer to the lord of Imola, or a pope, or a Roman emperor. In the end, as far as possible, I have resolved this problem by using the rather unattractive word 'ruler', or even the more generic 'leader', though always making it clear that we're talking about the political leader of a state. The book's famous title, however, must be left as it is.

Even harder to solve is the translation of *'virtù'*, together with a number of other words that cluster round it. It would be so easy to write the English cognate 'virtue', meaning the opposite of vice, but this is not what Machiavelli was talking about. He was not interested in the polarity 'good'/'evil', but in winning and losing, strength and weakness, success and failure. For Machiavelli '*virtù*' was any quality of character that enabled you to take political power or to hold on to it; in short, a winning trait. It could be courage in battle, or strength of personality, or political cunning, or it might even be the kind of ruthless cruelty that lets your subjects know you mean business. But one can hardly write 'cunning' or 'cruelty' for '*virtù*', even if one knows that in this context that is what the text means; because then you would lose the sense that although Machiavelli is not talking about the moral virtues he nevertheless wants to give a positive connotation to the particular qualities he is talking about: this cruelty is aimed at solving problems, retaining power, keeping a state strong, hence, in this context it is a '*virtù*'.

Ugly though it may sound, then, I have sometimes been obliged to translate '*virtù*' as 'positive qualities' or 'strength of character', except of course on those occasions – because there are some – when Machiavelli does mean 'virtues' in the moral sense: in which case he's usually talking about the importance of faking them even if you may not have them. Faking, of course, when cunningly deployed for an appropriate end, is another important *virtù*. The spin doctor was not a notion invented in the 1990s.

Related to both these particular problems – prince, virtue – is the more general difficulty that so many of the key words Machiavelli uses have English cognates through Latin – *fortuna, audace, circospetto, malignità, diligente*, etc. In some cases they are true cognates – *prudente*/prudent, for example – but even then to use the cognate pulls us back to a rather dusty, archaic style. Aren't the words 'careful' or 'cautious' or 'considered' more often used now than the word 'prudent'? Something of the same difficulty can occur where there is no cognate in English but a traditional and consolidated dictionary equivalent for an old Italian term. Machiavelli frequently uses the word '*savio*', which has usually been translated 'wise', but again this invites the English version to drift towards that slightly stilted archaic style so often used to render great texts from the past; 'sensible' or on other occasions 'shrewd' are choices that, depending on the context, can combine accuracy with a prose that draws less attention to itself as a translation.

So the constantly recurring question as one translates *The Prince* is: what words would we use today to describe the qualities and situations Machiavelli is talking about? Of course sometimes there are no modern words, because there are certain things – siege engines, cavalry attacks – that we don't talk about any more. On the whole, though, Machiavelli is chiefly interested in psychology or, rather, in the interaction of different personalities in crisis situations, and here, so long as the translator avoids the temptation to introduce misleading contemporary jargon, a great deal can be done to get *The Prince* into clear, contemporary English.

However, the difficulty of these lexical choices is infinitely compounded by Machiavelli's wayward grammar and extremely flexible syntax. Written in 1513, *The Prince* is not easily comprehensible to Italians today. Recent editions of the work are usually parallel texts with a modern Italian translation printed beside the original. The obstacle for the Italian reader, however, is hardly lexical at all – in the end he can understand a good ninety per cent of the words Machiavelli is using – rather it has to do with a combination of extreme compression of thought, obsolete, sometimes erratic grammar, and, above all, a syntax where subordinate and pre-modifying clauses abound in ways that the modern reader is not used to.

We are not talking here about those complex but always elegant Ciceronian sentences so admired and frequently mimicked by the English Augustans. Machiavelli has a more spoken, flexible, persuading, sometimes brusque voice, and to get that tone in English one has to opt for a syntax that is quite different from the original Italian. In particular, the sequence with which information is delivered within the sentence frequently has to be reorganized. Here, to give the reader a sense of what he can expect, are three versions of the same paragraph, the last being my own. I haven't chosen anything especially complex; it's a fairly ordinary passage in which, as so often, Machiavelli poses a situation, then considers possible responses to it and the consequences of each response. The first translation is from W. K. Marriot and was published in 1908.

> A prince is also respected when he is either a true friend or a downright enemy, that is to say, when, without any reservation, he declares himself in favour of one party against the other; which course will always be more advantageous than standing neutral; because if two of your powerful neighbours come to blows, they are of such a character that, if one of them conquers, you have either to fear him or not. In either case it will always be more advantageous for you to declare yourself and to make war strenuously; because, in the first case, if you do not declare yourself, you will invariably fall a prey to the conqueror, to the pleasure and satisfaction of him who has been conquered, and you will have no reasons to offer, nor anything to protect or to shelter you. Because he who conquers does not want doubtful friends who will not aid him in the time of trial; and he who loses will not harbour you because you did not willingly, sword in hand, court his fate.

The second is from George Bull, published in 1961.

> A prince also wins prestige for being a true friend or a true enemy, that is, for revealing himself without any reservation

in favour of one side against another. This policy is always
more advantageous than neutrality. For instance, if the powers
neighbouring on you come to blows, either they are such that,
if one of them conquers, you will be in danger, or they are not.
In either case it will always be to your advantage to declare
yourself and to wage a vigorous war; because, in the first case,
if you do not declare yourself you will always be at the mercy
of the conqueror, much to the pleasure and satisfaction of the
one who has been beaten, and you will have no justification
nor any way to obtain protection or refuge. The conqueror
does not want doubtful friends who do not help him when he
is in difficulties; the loser repudiates you because you were
unwilling to go, arms in hand, and throw in your lot with him.

And here is my own.

A ruler will also be respected when he is a genuine friend and
a genuine enemy, that is, when he declares himself unambiguously for one side and against the other. This policy will always
bring better results than neutrality. For example, if you have
two powerful neighbours who go to war, you may or may not
have reason to fear the winner afterwards. Either way it will
always be better to take sides and fight hard. If you do have
cause to fear but stay neutral, you'll still be gobbled up by the
winner to the amusement and satisfaction of the loser; you'll
have no excuses, no defence and nowhere to hide. Because a
winner doesn't want half-hearted friends who don't help him
in a crisis; and the loser will have nothing to do with you since
you didn't choose to fight alongside him and share his fate.

A typically tricky moment in this passage comes when
Machiavelli says of these neighbouring powers:

... o sono di qualità che, vincendo uno di quelli, tu abbia a
temere del vincitore, o no.

Literally:

> ... either they are of qualities that, winning one of those, you
> ought to fear the winner, or not.

Here Marriot gives:

> ... they are of such a character that, if one of them conquers,
> you have either to fear him or not.

And Bull:

> ... either they are such that, if one of them conquers, you will
> be in danger, or they are not.

Here it's clear that Bull is closer to modern prose, yet one
still feels that nobody writing down this idea today in English
would introduce the second part of Machiavelli's alternative
as Bull does by tagging that 'or they are not' on to the end of
the sentence after the introduction of an 'if' clause. If we
follow Bull's general structure but move the alternative forward – thus, 'either they are or they aren't such that if one of
them conquers, you will be in danger' – the sentence gains in
fluency. In the end, however, the simplest solution seemed to
me to shift the alternative aspect towards the verb 'fear' and
away from a description of the two states; this leaves the
sense of the sentence intact and allows us to get closer to
the original's telegraphic delivery.

> ... you may or may not have reason to fear the winner
> afterwards.

Let me say at this point that I have the greatest respect for
both these earlier translations and indeed various others. I
owe a lot to them, because, although I have always translated

directly from the original, I have then gone to these and to the modern Italian translations to see where they disagree and to mull over what I can learn from them. The original text is such that on occasion all four of the translations I have been looking at, two English and two Italian, offer different interpretations. In these cases one really must attune oneself to Machiavelli's mental processes, his insistence on logic, reason and deduction, and remember that every clause, if not every word, is there for a purpose.

Here is a small example. Having stated that rulers must at all costs avoid being hated by their subjects, and that such hatred is almost always the cause of a leader's downfall, Machiavelli foresees that some people will object that this wasn't the case with many Roman emperors who either held on to power despite being hated by the people, or lost it despite being loved. 'To meet these objections', he tells us, 'I shall consider the qualities of some of these emperors, showing how the causes of their downfall are not at all out of line with my reasoning above.' So far so good, but this sentence then ends:

> . . . e parte metterò in considerazione quelle cose che sono notabili a chi legge le azioni di quelli tempi.

Translating word for word, this gives:

> . . . and part I will put in consideration those things that are important to people who read the events of those times.

What is this about? Why did Machiavelli feel the need to add these words to a sentence that already seems clear enough. Bull offers:

> . . . I shall submit for consideration examples which are well known to students of the period.

This may sound sensible and vaguely academic, but it simply isn't accurate: the word '*parte*' has gone; to 'submit for consideration' may be a standard English formula, but does it mean the same as Machiavelli's actually rather unusual 'put in consideration'? '*Notabile*' doesn't so much mean 'well known' as 'worthy of note' or 'important'. Marriot gives:

> . . . at the same time I will only submit for consideration those things that are noteworthy to him who studies the affairs of those times.

Again we have the standard 'submit for consideration', while 'at the same time' and 'only' are both translator's additions. It now sounds as if Machiavelli is reassuring us that he will only look at examples that are relevant, but this sort of defensiveness is not the author's way. Why would the reader have suspected him of introducing irrelevant examples?

One modern Italian translation gives: 'e in parte indicherò quei fatti che sono importanti per chi si interessa alla storia di quei tempi.' Literally: 'and in part I will indicate those facts that are important for people interested in the history of those times.'

This is now extremely close to our literal translation of Machiavelli's original but still not particularly helpful. What is the author getting at? What does the phrase add to what has already been said?

Another Italian translation gives: 'nello stesso tempo indicherò i fatti che devono essere messi in evidenza da chi si interessa alla storia di quei tempi.' Literally: 'at the same time I will indicate the facts that must be put in evidence by people interested in the history of those times.'

Despite the fact that '*parte*' has once again been mysteriously transformed into 'at the same time' – a classic filler when a translator is lost – an idea at last emerges: that there are facts that people interested in those times 'must put in evidence', and the implication is that without these facts we won't understand what has to be understood if we are to be persuaded by the author's argument.

At this point the translator tries to enter Machiavelli's reasoning, reassured by the knowledge that here we have an author who *always* put sense and clarity before anything else. Machiavelli, remember, is facing objections from people who claim that the question of whether a ruler's people do or do not hate him is not the crucial criterion when it comes to considering whether that leader will survive. Those objections, what's more, are based on the lives of certain Roman emperors. What Machiavelli is going to show in the following paragraphs is that the nature of power and political institutions in the Roman empire was profoundly different from that in a modern (early sixteenth-century) state, the key difference being the existence, in Roman times, of a strong standing army that, for safety's sake, a leader had to satisfy *before* satisfying the people and that could often only be kept happy by allowing it to treat the people very harshly, stealing and raping at will. What this little clause appears to be doing, then, is preparing us for Machiavelli's approach to answering the objection that has been raised: it is a question, he is going to tell us, of understanding a different historical context.

The word '*parte*' could be short for '*a parte*' (apart, separately) or '*in parte*' (in part), as both the Italian translations take it. Now perhaps we can read the sentence as a whole thus:

> To meet these objections, I shall consider the qualities of some of these emperors, showing how the causes of their downfall are not at all out of line with my reasoning above, and bringing into the argument some of the context that historians of the period consider important.

The original '*mettere in considerazione*' ('put in consideration') is used only once in the whole of *The Prince* (having the text in electronic form is a huge help to the translator), hence the decision not to translate with a standard formula such as 'submit for consideration', but to give a more precise sense to the words with the expression 'bringing into the argument': Machiavelli is advising us that for these particular examples he will have to fill in a different context. The idea of '*parte*' I have understood as 'in part', and then for the sake of fluency rendered it with 'some': the author can't bring in all the context, but some of it.

One has no way of knowing whether this is exactly what Machiavelli meant, but the sentence now gives an internal cohesion to the passage that was lacking in other versions. And if we return to our word-for-word translation of the original – 'and part I will put in consideration those things that are important to people who read the events of those times' – we see that it can indeed be read in the way we have chosen to render it.

One particularly pernicious problem a translator faces as he grapples with *The Prince* is the book's reputation. Machiavelli is a scandal, every schoolboy knows, because he puts the ends before the means to the point of condoning acts of violence, cruelty and betrayal, something Christian and modern western ethics consider unacceptable: we don't condone a brutal killing just because it puts an end to a riot and we are no longer at ease with the idea of torture, even when it might prevent a terrorist atrocity. The climax of this scandal comes with the author's discussion of Cesare Borgia, a man who rose to power and kept it with the use of extraordinary treachery and cruelty. The temptation for the translator is to play to the reputation of the book, underlining Machiavelli's extreme views and making sure the text doesn't 'disappoint', even when its tone and subtlety are not, perhaps, exactly what readers were expecting.

At the end of the discussion of Borgia, having recounted

how he eventually lost power when his father, Pope Alexander, suddenly and unexpectedly died and a pope hostile to Borgia was elected, Machiavelli writes: 'Raccolte io adunque tutte le azioni del duca, non saprei riprenderlo.' Literally, we have: 'Having gathered then all the actions of the duke, I would not know how to reproach him.'

Bull gives: 'So having summed up all that the duke did, I cannot possibly censure him.' Here the word 'censure' has a strong moral connotation, and the statement is made stronger still by the introduction of 'can't possibly', which seems a heavy interpretation of the standard Italian formula 'I wouldn't know how to'. In Bull's version it seems that Machiavelli is making a point of telling us that he has no moral objections to anything Cesare Borgia did, this in line with the author's reputation for cynicism.

Marriot more cautiously gives: 'When all the actions of the duke are recalled, I do not know how to blame him', and both Italian translations take the same line. The fact is that just as the word '*virtù*' is rarely used in a strictly moral context, so the word '*riprendere*', 'reproach', refers not to moral behaviour, but to the question: did the duke get something wrong, did he make a mistake? A key to reading the word comes at the opening to the next paragraph where we have: 'Solamente si può accusarlo nella creazione di Iulio pontefice, nella quale lui ebbe mala elezione', which, more or less literally, gives us: 'The only thing Borgia can be accused of is his role in the election of Pope Julius, where he made a bad choice' (that is, as far as his own interests were concerned, he backed the wrong man).

Here we approach the subtler scandal of Machiavelli's text: it is not that the author is *insisting* that Borgia's immoral acts should not be censured, rather that Machiavelli is just not interested in discussing the moral aspect of the question at all, or not from a Christian point of view. For him it is a case of shrewd or mistaken choices, not of good or evil. When he proposes Borgia as a model, neither morality nor immorality come into it, only the fact that this man knew how to win power and hold it and build a strong state.

Finally, one can't help noticing a certain Victorian bashfulness in previous translations. Machiavelli was a notorious womanizer and in writing *The Prince* he believed he was addressing an audience of men who had no worries about political correctness. When he says 'la fortuna è donna, et è necessario, volendola tenere sotto, batterla et urtarla' – literally: 'fortune is woman and it is necessary wanting to keep her underneath to beat her and shove her' – there is an obvious sexual reference. The phrase comes in the last paragraph of *The Prince* proper (the closing exhortation is very much a piece apart) and Machiavelli wants to go out on a strong but, as he no doubt saw it, witty note.

Here is Marriot's version of the whole last paragraph:

> I conclude, therefore, that fortune being changeful and mankind steadfast in their ways, so long as the two are in agreement men are successful, but unsuccessful when they fall out. For my part I consider that it is better to be adventurous than cautious, because fortune is a woman, and if you wish to keep her under it is necessary to beat and ill-use her; and it is seen that she allows herself to be mastered by the adventurous rather than by those who go to work more coldly. She is, therefore, always, woman-like, a lover of young men, because they are less cautious, more violent, and with more audacity command her.

And Bull's:

> I conclude, therefore, that as fortune is changeable whereas men are obstinate in their ways, men prosper so long as fortune and policy are in accord, and where there is a clash they fail.

I hold strongly to this: that it is better to be impetuous than
circumspect; because fortune is a woman and if she is to be
submissive it is necessary to beat and coerce her. Experience
shows that she is more often subdued by men who do this than
by those who act coldly. Always, being a woman, she favours
young men, because they are less circumspect and more ardent,
and because they command her with greater audacity.

I hope I am getting closer to the spirit of the thing and, for
better or worse, the kind of man Machiavelli was, offering
this:

To conclude then: fortune varies but men go on regardless.
When their approach suits the times they're successful, and
when it doesn't they're not. My opinion on the matter is this:
it's better to be impulsive than cautious; fortune is female and
if you want to stay on top of her you have to slap and thrust.
You'll see she's more likely to yield that way than to men who
go about her coldly. And being a woman she likes her men
young, because they're not so cagey, they're wilder and more
daring when they master her.

Italy in 1500

THE PRINCE

Letter to Lorenzo de' Medici

People trying to attract the good will of a sovereign usually offer him something they care a lot about themselves, or something they've seen he particularly likes. So rulers are always being given horses, arms, gold brocades, jewels and whatever finery seems appropriate. Eager myself to bring Your Highness some token of my loyalty, I realized there was nothing more precious or important to me than my knowledge of great men and their doings, a knowledge gained through long experience of contemporary affairs and a constant study of ancient history. Having thought over all I've learned, and analysed it with the utmost care, I've written everything down in a short book that I am now sending to Your Highness.

And though this gift is no doubt unworthy of you, I feel sure the experience it contains will make it welcome, especially when you think that I could hardly offer anything better than the chance to grasp in a few hours what I have discovered and assimilated over many years of danger and discomfort. I haven't prettified the book or padded it out with long sentences or pompous, pretentious words, or any of the irrelevant flourishes and attractions so many writers use; I didn't want it to please for anything but the range and seriousness of its subject matter. Nor, I hope, will you think it presumptuous that a man of low, really the lowest, station should set out to discuss the way princes ought to govern their peoples. Just as artists who draw landscapes get down in the valley to study the mountains and go up to the mountains to look down on the valley, so one has to be a prince to get to know the character of a people and a man of the people to know the character of a prince.

Your Highness, please take this small gift in the spirit in which it is given. Study it carefully and you will find that my most earnest wish is that you should achieve the greatness that your status and qualities promise. Then if, from the high peak of your position, you ever look down on those far below, you will see how very ungenerously and unfairly life continues to treat me.

I

Different kinds of states and how to conquer them

All states and governments that ever ruled over men have been either republics or monarchies. Monarchies may be hereditary, if the ruler's family has governed for generations, or new. New monarchies can either be entirely new, as when Francesco Sforza captured Milan, or they could be territories a ruler has added to his existing hereditary state by conquest, as when the King of Spain took Naples. An additional territory won by conquest will be accustomed either to living under a monarch or to the freedom of self-government and may be conquered by the new ruler's own army or that of a third party, by luck or deservedly.

2

Hereditary monarchies

I won't be considering republics since I've written about them at length elsewhere. Instead I'll concentrate on monarchies, taking the situations mentioned above and discussing how each kind of state can best be governed and held.

So I'll begin by noting that hereditary monarchies where people have long been used to the ruler's family are far easier to hold than new ones; all a monarch need do is avoid upsetting the order established by his predecessors, trim policies to circumstances when there is trouble, and, assuming he is of average ability, he will keep his kingdom for life. Only extraordinary and overwhelming force will be able to take it off him and even then he'll win it back as soon as the occupying power runs into trouble.

An example of this situation in Italy is the Duchy of Ferrara. In 1484 and 1510 the Duchy was briefly conquered by foreign powers, first the Venetians, then Pope Julius, but these defeats had nothing to do with the territory's having a well-established ruling family. A ruler who inherits power has less reason or need to upset his subjects than a new one and as a result is better loved. If he doesn't go out of his way to get himself hated, it's reasonable to suppose his people will wish him well. When a dynasty survives for generations memories fade and likewise motives for change; upheaval, on the contrary, always leaves the scaffolding for building further change.

3

Mixed monarchies

When a monarchy is new, things are harder. If it's not entirely new but a territory added to an existing monarchy (let's call this overall situation 'mixed') instabilities are caused first and foremost by what is an inevitable problem for all new regimes: that men are quick to change ruler when they imagine they can improve their lot – it is this conviction that prompts them to take up arms and rebel – then later they discover they were wrong and that things have got worse rather than better. Again this is in the normal, natural way of things: a ruler is bound to upset the people in his new territories, first with his occupying army and then with all the endless injustices consequent on any invasion. So not only do you make enemies of those whose interests you damaged when you occupied the territory, but you can't even keep the friendship of the people who helped you to take power, this for the simple reason that you can't give them as much as they expected. And you can't get tough with them either, since you still need them; because however strong your armies, you'll always need local support to occupy a new territory. This is why Louis XII, King of France, took Milan so quickly and equally quickly lost it. The first time this happened Duke Ludovico was able to retake the city with his own forces, because the people who had previously opened the gates to Louis saw their mistake, realized they wouldn't be getting the benefits they'd hoped for and didn't want to submit to the harsh conditions imposed by the new king.

Of course, when a king returns to win back a territory that has rebelled like this, he is less likely to lose it a second time. Having learned from the rebellion, he'll have fewer scruples when it comes to punishing troublemakers, interrogating suspects and strengthening any weak points in his defences. So while the first time Louis invaded Milan it took no more than a little sword-rattling along the borders from Ludovico to force a retreat, the second time it would take the whole world to defeat his armies and drive them out of Italy. This for the reasons listed above. All the same, they were driven out both times.

The general reasons behind the first French defeat have been discussed. It remains to explain why Louis lost Milan the second time and to see what counter-measures he could have taken and what options a ruler has in a situation like this if he wants to hold on to his conquest.

Needless to say, any territory annexed to the realm of a conquering ruler may or may not be in the same geographical region and share the same language. If it is and the language is shared, the territory will be much easier to hold on to, especially if its people are not used to the freedom of self-government. In that case all you have to do is eliminate the family of the previous ruler and your hold on power is guaranteed. Everything else in the territory can then be left as it was and, given that there are no profound differences in customs, people will accept the situation quietly enough. Certainly this has proved true in Burgundy, Brittany, Gascony and Normandy, all of which have now been under French rule for many years. Even where there is some difference in language, the customs of these territories are similar and people can get along with each other. So a ruler who has taken territories in these circumstances must have two priorities: first, to eliminate the family of the previous rulers; second, to leave all laws and taxes as they were. In this way the acquired territory and the king's original possessions will soon form a single entity.

But when a ruler occupies a state in an area that has a different language, different customs and different institutions, then things get tough. To hold on to a new possession in these circumstances takes a lot of luck and hard work. Perhaps the most effective solution is for the new ruler to go and live there himself. This will improve security and make the territory more stable. The Turkish sultan did this in Greece, and all the other measures he took to hold on to the country would have been ineffective if he hadn't. When you're actually there, you can see when things start going wrong and nip rebellion in the bud; when you're far away you only find out about it when it's too late. Another advantage is that the new territory won't be plundered by your officials. Its subjects will be happy that they can appeal to a ruler who is living among them. So, if they're intending to be obedient, they'll have one more reason to love you, and if they're not, all the more reason to fear you. Anyone planning an attack from outside will think twice about it. So, if you go and live in the new territory you've taken, you're very unlikely to lose it.

Another good solution is to establish colonies in one or two places. These work rather like chains to bind the captured state to your own. If you don't do this you'll have to keep large numbers of infantry and cavalry in the territory. Colonies don't cost a great deal. You can send and maintain them very cheaply and they only arouse the hostility of the people whose houses and land are expropriated to give to the colonists. Since that will only be a very small proportion of the population, and since these people will now be poor and will have fled to different places, they can hardly cause much trouble. Everyone else will be unaffected (hence prone to keep quiet) and at the same time frightened of stepping out of line for fear of having their own houses and land taken away. In conclusion, colonies are cheap, more loyal, provoke less hostility among your new subjects, and, as I've said, those few who are provoked can't fight back since they'll be dispossessed refugees. In this regard it's worth noting that in general you must either pamper people or destroy them; harm them just a little and they'll hit back; harm them seriously and they won't be able to. So if you're going to do people harm, make sure you needn't worry about their reaction. If, on the other hand, you decide to send an occupying army rather than establish colonies, the operation will be far more expensive and all the revenues from the new territory will be used up in defending it, turning what should have been a gain into a loss. And you'll provoke more hostility: an army moving about and requisitioning lodgings will do damage across the entire territory, something that has consequences for the whole population and turns them all into enemies. And these are enemies who can hit back, people beaten but still on their own ground. So however you look at it military garrisons are as pointless as colonies are useful.

A ruler who has moved into a new region with a different language and customs must also make himself leader and protector of the weaker neighbouring powers, while doing what he can to undermine the stronger. In particular, he must take care that no foreign power strong enough to compete with his own gets a chance to penetrate the area. People who are discontented, whether out of fear or frustrated ambition, will always encourage a foreign power to intervene. It was the Aetolians who invited the Romans into Greece. Every time the Romans moved into a new region it was on the invitation of local people. And it's in the nature of things that as soon as a powerful foreign ruler moves into a region, all the weaker local powers support him, if only out of resentment towards the stronger states that previously kept them down. So the new ruler will have no trouble winning their support; they'll all run to ally themselves with the territory he has taken. He just has to watch out that they don't grab too much power and authority. Then, with his own strength and their support, he can easily undermine the more powerful neighbours and hence dominate the region. However, an invader who fails to manage relations with his new neighbours will soon lose what territory he has taken; and even while he's still holding on to it, he'll be up against all kinds of trouble and hostility.

The Romans followed these principles whenever they took a new province: they sent colonists; they established friendly relations with weaker neighbours, though without allowing them to increase their power; they undermined stronger neighbours and they prevented powerful rulers outside the region from gaining influence there. Their handling of Greece will be example enough: they established good relations with the Achaeans and the Aetolians; Macedonia's power was undermined; they drove out Antiochus. They didn't reward the good behaviour of the Achaeans and the Aetolians by allowing them any new territory and whenever Philip convinced them to establish friendly relations with him they made sure he was weakened as a result. Antiochus, for all his strength, was never allowed any influence in the region. The Romans were simply doing what all wise rulers must: not restricting themselves to dealing with present threats but using every means at their disposal to foresee and forestall future problems as well. Seen in advance, trouble is easily dealt with; wait until it's on top of you and your reaction will come too late, the malaise is already irreversible.

Remember what the doctors tell us about tuberculosis: in its early stages it's easy to cure and hard to diagnose, but if you don't spot it and treat it, as time goes by it gets easy to diagnose and hard to cure. So it is with affairs of state. See trouble in advance (but you have to be shrewd) and you can clear it up quickly. Miss it, and by the time it's big enough for everyone to see it will be too late to do anything about it.

However, since they had this capacity for seeing a threat in advance, the Romans always knew how to respond. They never put off a war when they saw trouble coming; they knew it couldn't be avoided in the long run and that the odds would simply shift in favour of their enemies. They chose to fight Philip and Antiochus in Greece, so as not to have to fight them in Italy. They could have put off both wars, but they didn't. They never took the line our pundits are constantly giving us today – relax, time is on your side – but rather they put their faith in their own foresight and spirit. Time hurries everything on and can just as easily make things worse as better.

But let's get back to the King of France and see if he took any of the measures we've been discussing. And when I say the King, I mean Louis, not Charles, since Louis held territory in Italy for longer than Charles and it's easier to see what his methods were. You'll notice that he did the opposite of what a ruler must do to hold on to conquests in a region whose customs and language differ from those of his home kingdom.

It was Venetian ambitions that brought Louis into Italy. The Venetians planned to take half of Lombardy while he seized the other half. I'm not going to criticize Louis for agreeing to this. He wanted to get a first foothold in Italy, he didn't have any friends in the region – on the contrary, thanks to King Charles's behaviour before him, all doors were barred – so he was forced to accept what allies he found. And the arrangement would have worked if he hadn't made mistakes in other departments. Taking Lombardy, the king recovered in one blow the reputation that Charles had lost. Genoa surrendered. The Florentines offered an alliance. The Marquis of Mantua, the Duke of Ferrara, Bentivogli of Bologna, Caterina Sforza of Forlì, the lords of Faenza, Pesaro, Rimini, Camerino and Piombino, as well as the republics of Lucca, Pisa and Siena, all queued up to make friends. At which point the Venetians were in a position to see how rash they had been when they proposed the initial deal: for two towns in Lombardy they had made Louis king over a third of Italy.

Think how easily Louis could have held on to his position in Italy if he had observed the rules outlined above and guaranteed security and protection to all those friends. There were so many of them and they were so weak and frightened, either of Venice or Rome, that they were simply forced to side with Louis. Then with their help he could easily have defended himself against the states that were still powerful. But no sooner had he arrived in Milan than Louis did the opposite; he helped Pope Alexander to invade Romagna. He didn't see that this decision weakened his own position, losing him friends and the support of those who had run to him for help, while reinforcing the pope, adding temporal dominion to the spiritual power that already gives a pope so much authority. Having made that first mistake, he was dragged in deeper, since, to curb Alexander's ambitions and prevent him from taking control of Tuscany, he was forced to advance further into Italy himself. Not content with having lost his friends and increased the power of the Church, he was eager now to get hold of the Kingdom of Naples and so made an agreement to split it with the King of Spain. Until then Louis had been the dominant power in Italy, but this move introduced another equally great power into the peninsula, with the result that anyone in the region who had ambitions or was disgruntled with Louis now had someone else to turn to. Louis could have kept Naples under a client king but instead he kicked the man out and brought in a king who was powerful enough to kick him out.

The desire to conquer more territory really is a very natural, ordinary thing and whenever men have the resources to do so they'll always be praised, or at least not blamed. But when they don't have the resources, yet carry on regardless, then they're at fault and deserve what blame they get. If Louis was in a position to capture the Kingdom of Naples with his own forces, then he should have gone ahead and done it; if he wasn't, he certainly shouldn't have split the territory with another king. Sharing Lombardy with the Venetians was forgivable, in that it gave him a foothold in Italy; but there was nothing necessary about sharing Naples with Spain and hence it was a mistake.

So Louis made five mistakes: he eliminated the weaker states; he enhanced the power of one of Italy's stronger states; he brought in an extremely powerful foreign king; he didn't go to live in the territory he'd acquired and he didn't establish colonies there.

All the same, these mistakes might not have done serious damage during his lifetime had he not now made a sixth by stripping Venice of its power. Of course, if he hadn't increased the pope's power and brought Spain into Italy, it would have been quite reasonable and even necessary to cut the Venetians down to size. But having taken those earlier decisions, he should never have reduced Venice to such a state of weakness. As long as Venice was militarily strong, no one else was going to try to take Lombardy from the French; the Venetians wouldn't have allowed another state to attack the region unless they were going to get territory themselves and the other states would never have wanted to take Lombardy from France if it meant giving it to Venice; plus, they would never have had the courage to confront France and Venice together. Someone might object: but Louis gave Romagna to Pope Alexander and Naples to Spain to avoid war; in which case, let me repeat what I said earlier: you must never fail to respond to trouble just to avoid war, because in the end you won't avoid it, you'll just be putting it off to your enemy's advantage. Someone else might insist that Louis had promised the pope he would attack Venice on his behalf in return for the pope's granting the French king a divorce and making the Archbishop of Rouen a cardinal; in this case let me refer the reader to what I'll be saying later about when rulers should, or then again shouldn't, keep their promises.

So Louis lost Lombardy because he didn't take the measures

others have taken when they conquered territory and were determined to hold on to it. There's nothing mysterious about this; it's all very normal and reasonable. In fact I discussed the matter in Nantes with the Cardinal of Rouen when Duke Valentino (that was what people used to call Cesare Borgia, Pope Alexander's son) was invading Romagna; and when the cardinal told me that the Italians knew nothing about war, I told him that the French knew nothing about politics, because if they did they wouldn't be letting the pope grow so powerful. And as it turned out, it was Rome and Spain, the two states whose power in Italy France had built up, that proved France's downfall. From which we can infer a general rule that always holds, or almost always: that to help another ruler to grow powerful is to prepare your own ruin; because it takes flair or military strength to build up a new power, and both will seem threatening to the person who has benefited from them.

4

Conquered by Alexander the Great, the Kingdom of Darius did not rebel against his successors after his death. Why not?

Now that we've seen how difficult it is to hold on to recently acquired territory some readers will be surprised to recall what happened when Alexander the Great conquered Asia in just a few years, then died very soon after his victory was complete. You would have thought the whole area would have rebelled, yet Alexander's successors held on to it and the only trouble they had arose from their own personal ambitions and infighting. To explain this situation let's start by remembering that all monarchies on record have been governed in one of two ways: either by a king and the servants he appoints as ministers to run his kingdom; or by a king and a number of barons, who are not appointed by the king but hold their positions thanks to hereditary privilege. These barons have their own lands and their own subjects who recognize the barons as their masters and are naturally loyal to them. Where a state is governed by a king and his ministers the king is more powerful since he is the only person in the state whom people recognize as superior. When they obey someone else it is only because he is a minister or official and they have no special loyalty to him.

Examples of these two forms of government in our own times are Turkey and France. The whole of Turkey is governed by one ruler, or sultan. Everyone serves him. He divides his realm into provinces, or *sanjaks*, and sends administrators to run them, appointing and dismissing them as he sees fit.

The King of France, on the other hand, is surrounded by any number of barons whose rights date back to ancient times and who are acknowledged and loved by their subjects. Each baron has specific privileges which a king can only take away at his peril. Looking at these two kinds of states, it's clear that Turkey is hard to conquer but once conquered very easy to hold. France on the other hand will be somewhat easier to conquer but very hard to hold.

The reason why it's hard to conquer a country like Turkey is that there are no barons to invite you in and you can't expect anyone to make your invasion easier by rebelling against the king. This follows naturally from the situation as described above; since all subjects are the king's servants and indebted to him it's hard to corrupt them, and even assuming you do manage to bribe someone he's not likely to be much help because he can't bring any local people along with him, this again for the reasons I've explained. So, anyone attacking this kind of country has to reckon that he will find it united against him and hence has to rely on his own armed forces rather than on any mutiny in enemy ranks. But once you have won and routed the enemy and made sure he can't rebuild his armies, then the only thing to worry about is the king and his family. Eliminate them and no one else can threaten you since no one commands the loyalty of the people. Just as before your victory you couldn't look to any barons for help, so after it there are none around to pose a threat.

The opposite is true in countries run along French lines. Here you can make inroads easily enough, winning the support of a baron or two. There's always someone unhappy with the king and eager for change. Then these people are well placed to get you a foothold in the country and help you to victory. But afterwards you're going to have all kinds of problems holding on to what you've won, problems with the people who fought on your side and problems with those who fought against you and lost. This time it won't be enough to eliminate the king's family because there will always be barons ready to assume authority when circumstances swing their way, and, since you can never give them everything they want and never eliminate them all, you'll lose the territory you took as soon as your enemies get an opportunity to rebel.

If we go back now to the Kingdom of Darius, we'll find that it was of the Turkish variety. So Alexander first had to defeat its entire army and get control of the country; but once he'd done that, and once Darius was dead, he was securely in command for the reasons cited above. And if his successors had been united they could have run the region without any worries; in fact the only trouble was the infighting they started themselves. But states organized the French way can never be held so easily. The frequent uprisings against Roman power in Spain, Gaul and Greece, for example, were the result of those regions' being internally divided into so many princi-palities. So long as people remembered their old loyalties to local lords, Rome was never in complete control. But once the power and permanence of empire had extinguished those loyalties, then Rome became the undisputed master of the region. In fact, when the Romans started fighting among themselves, each warring commander was able to bring the province he was running into the conflict on his side, since once the families of the old local rulers had been eliminated the only authority people recognized was Rome's representa-tive. When you take all this into account, it's really not sur-prising how easy it was for Alexander to hold Asia, nor how hard it was for many others, Pyrrhus for example, to hold on to the territories they took. It wasn't a question of the abilities of each particular conqueror, but of the different kinds of state they had invaded.

5

How to govern cities and states that were previously self-governing

When the states you invade have been accustomed to governing themselves without a monarch and living in freedom under their own laws, then there are three ways of holding on to them: the first is to reduce them to rubble; the second is to go and live there yourself; the third is to let them go on living under their own laws, make them pay you a tax and install a government of just a few local people to keep the state as a whole friendly. Since this government has been set up by the invading ruler, its members know they can't survive without his support and will do everything they can to defend his authority. Once you've decided not to destroy it, the best way to hold a previously self-governing city is with the help of its own citizens.

Let's take our examples from Sparta and Rome. The Spartans held Athens and Thebes by setting up governments run by a few local people, but in the end they lost these towns. The Romans razed Capua, Carthage and Numantia to the ground and that way held on to them. They tried to hold Greece in much the same way the Spartans had, granting it self-government and leaving it its own laws, but it didn't work and eventually they were forced to destroy quite a number of cities so as to keep hold of the region as a whole.

The truth is that the only sure way to hold such places is to destroy them. If you conquer a city accustomed to self-government and opt not to destroy it you can expect it to destroy you. Rebelling, its people will always rally to the cry of freedom and the inspiration of their old institutions. It doesn't matter how long they've been occupied or how benevolent the occupation, these things will never be forgotten. Whatever you do, whatever measures you take, if the population hasn't been routed and dispersed so that its freedoms and traditions are quite forgotten, they will rise up to fight for those principles at the first opportunity; just as the Pisans did after a hundred years of Florentine dominion.

But when a people has been accustomed to living under a ruler and the ruler's family has been eliminated, then, since they're used to obeying but now have no one to follow, they won't be able to choose a new leader from among themselves nor to live in freedom without one, so they'll be slower to rebel and an invader can win them over and gain their loyalty more easily. Republics, on the other hand, have more life in them, more hatred and a greater thirst for revenge. Their memory of old freedoms lingers on and won't let them rest. In these cases, your only options are to reduce the place to rubble or go and live there yourself.

6

States won by the new ruler's own forces and abilities

In the following discussion dealing with states where both the ruler and the form of government are entirely new, no one should be surprised if I choose to cite the most impressive examples. The fact is that although people almost always proceed by imitation, following in another man's footsteps, you can never tread a model's path or reproduce his qualities exactly. So, if you're sensible, you set out to follow a trail blazed by someone who was truly great, someone really worth imitating, so that even if you're not on the same level yourself at least you'll reflect a little of his brilliance. It's like the clever archer who senses that his target is too far off, knows the limitations of his bow, and so aims far higher than he normally would, not because he really wants his arrow to go that high, but to have it fall from a height on to his target.

So let's start by saying that when it comes to entirely new regimes where a new ruler has seized the state, the ease or difficulty of his staying in power will be in proportion to his abilities or failings. And since you can't go from being an ordinary citizen to a ruler without either talent or favourable circumstances, we must suppose that one or the other of these factors will be offsetting, at least in part, a great many difficulties. That said, those who haven't relied too much on lucky circumstances have lasted longer. Another positive factor is that since in this case the ruler doesn't already possess another state, he will be forced to live in his new territory.

But to turn to those who became rulers through their own qualities rather than by luck, no doubt the most impressive are: Moses, Cyrus, Romulus, Theseus and suchlike figures. And though we can hardly say much about Moses, since he merely carried out God's orders, all the same we have to admire him for the grace that made him worthy of God's attention. But let's look at Cyrus and other men who won and founded kingdoms. We'll find they are all admirable and when we look into the specific actions each took and the institutions they established, we'll see they don't differ that much from what Moses did under divine guidance. Analysing their lives and achievements, we notice that the only part luck played was in giving them an initial opportunity: they were granted the raw material and had the chance to mould it into whatever shape they wanted. Without this opportunity their talent would have gone unused, and without their talent the opportunity would have gone begging.

So, if Moses hadn't found the people of Israel in Egypt, enslaved and oppressed and in need of a leader to get them out of the situation, they would never have been willing to follow him. If Romulus hadn't been abandoned at birth and chosen to leave Alba Longa, how could he have become king and founder of Rome? If Cyrus hadn't found the Persians ready to rebel against the occupation of the Medes, and the Medes undisciplined and effeminate after a long period of peace, he couldn't have achieved what he did. And Theseus could hardly have shown his qualities if the Athenians hadn't first been defeated and dispersed. These opportunities made these men's fortunes and it was because of their remarkable qualities that they were able to recognize and grasp the opportunities, bringing glory and even greater good fortune to their countries.

These men and others like them who rise to sovereignty through their own abilities face all kinds of difficulties when setting up their states but then hold on to them fairly easily.

The initial difficulties depend in large part on the fact that in order to establish their government and guarantee its security they have to impose a new administrative system and new procedures. Here we have to bear in mind that nothing is harder to organize, more likely to fail, or more dangerous to see through, than the introduction of a new system of government. The person bringing in the changes will make enemies of everyone who was doing well under the old system, while the people who stand to gain from the new arrangements will not offer wholehearted support, partly because they are afraid of their opponents, who still have the laws on their side, and partly because people are naturally sceptical: no one really believes in change until they've had solid experience of it. So as soon as the opponents of the new system see a chance, they'll go on the offensive with the determination of an embattled faction, while its supporters will offer only half-hearted resistance, something that will put the new ruler's position at risk too.

To get a better grasp of the problem, we have to ask: is the leader introducing the changes relying on his own resources, or does he depend on other people's support; that is, does he have to beg help to achieve his goals, or can he impose them? If he's begging help, he's bound to fail and will get nowhere. But if he's got his own resources and can impose his plans, then it's unlikely he'll be running serious risks. This is why the visionary who has armed force on his side has always won through, while unarmed even your visionary is always a loser. Because on top of everything else, we must remember that the general public's mood will swing. It's easy to convince people of something, but hard to keep them convinced. So when they stop believing in you, you must be in a position to force them to believe.

Moses, Cyrus, Theseus and Romulus couldn't have got people to respect their new laws for long if they hadn't possessed armed force. We saw what happened in our own times to Girolamo Savonarola: he was overthrown along with all his reforms when people stopped believing in him. He had no way of keeping the initial believers on board or forcing the sceptical to see the light. But any new ruler bringing in changes will have to deal with huge obstacles and dangers, mostly in the early stages, and must overcome them with his own abilities. Once he's done that and eliminated those who resented his achievements, so that people start to respect and admire him, then he can enjoy his power in safety and will live honoured and fulfilled.

I've mentioned four exceptional leaders but now I want to bring in a lesser man, Hiero of Syracuse, who nevertheless had some of the same qualities as the others and will serve as an example of a whole category. Originally an ordinary citizen, Hiero became King of Syracuse. Once again the only luck he had lay in the initial situation: under threat from Carthage, the Syracusans elected him as their military commander and he was so successful they then made him king. In fact, even as a private citizen he was so capable that one writer said of him: 'He had all it takes to be a king except a kingdom.' Hiero disbanded the existing army and mustered a new one. He broke off old alliances and made new ones; that way, with his own soldiers and his own allies to support him, he had laid the foundation for building whatever he wanted. So it cost him considerable effort to establish his power, but very little to hold on to it.

7

States won by lucky circumstance and someone else's armed forces

A private citizen who becomes a ruler out of sheer good luck needn't make much effort to take his state but will have to sweat if he is to hold on to it. He has no trouble climbing on to his pedestal, since he is lifted there; but as soon as he is up on top, there will be any number of problems. I'm talking about situations where someone buys a territory with money, or is simply granted it as a favour. This was the case with quite a few rulers of cities in Ionia and the Hellespont: Darius gave them their thrones so that they would govern with his security and prestige in mind. Another example is those emperors who started out as private citizens and rose to power by bribing the army.

These men rely entirely on the support and continuing success of the people who gave them their power, which is to say on two extremely unreliable and unstable quantities. They don't know how to hang on to power and even if they did, they wouldn't be able to. They don't know how because, unless they are remarkably gifted and competent, we can hardly suppose that their lives as private citizens have equipped them for command. They won't be able to in any event because they don't possess an army that can be relied on to stay friendly and loyal. Like anything that appears suddenly and grows fast, regimes that come out of nothing inevitably have shallow roots and will tend to crash in the first storm. Unless of course the man who is suddenly made a ruler turns out to be so talented that he immediately sets to work to defend what luck has brought his way and to build the foundations that another leader would have established before coming to power.

I'd like to mention two men from our own times who achieved power in these different ways, one through his own abilities and one by luck. The people I have in mind are Francesco Sforza and Cesare Borgia. With the right policies and great courage, Sforza, a commoner, became Duke of Milan and, having won power with enormous effort, held on to it easily enough. Borgia, on the other hand, or Duke Valentino as he was commonly known, received his territories thanks to his father's position, and when his father died he lost them, this despite the fact that he used all means available and did everything a sensible, capable man could have done to lay the foundations for his own rule in the lands that another man's army and position had won for him. As we said earlier on, if you haven't laid the foundations before becoming king, it takes very special qualities to do it afterwards, and even then it'll be tough for the architect and risky for the building. If we look carefully at Borgia's strategies, we'll see that he did in fact lay down good foundations for future power; and I think it makes sense to discuss how he did it, because I wouldn't know what better advice to give a ruler new to power than to follow his example. If his efforts eventually came to nothing, it was not due to his own shortcomings, but to an extraordinary run of bad luck.

When Pope Alexander VI decided to turn his son into a powerful duke, he faced all kinds of obstacles, present and future. First, he couldn't see how he could make him ruler of anywhere that wasn't Church territory. But he knew that if he gave away Church land, the Duke of Milan and the Venetians would block him, since Faenza and Rimini were already under Venetian protection. What's more, the armies then operating in Italy, particularly those the pope might have called on for help, were all controlled by people – the Orsini, the Colonna and associated families – who had reason to fear papal expansionism, and hence couldn't be trusted. What Alexander had to do then was undermine the status quo and the authority of his rivals so as to seize control of part of their lands with impunity. This turned out to be easy because, for reasons all their own, the Venetians were now determined to bring the French back into Italy. Rather than opposing the move, the pope smoothed the way by dissolving King Louis's first marriage for him.

So the French king entered Italy with Venetian help and papal consent. No sooner had he taken Milan than the pope got the king to send troops to help his son, Borgia, take Romagna, something that would have been impossible without Louis's support. With the forces of the Colonna family now beaten, Borgia faced two obstacles if he was to hold on to Romagna and acquire further territory: the first was his own army, which he suspected of disloyalty; the second was French policy. Duke Valentino had been using the forces of the Orsini family but was afraid they would stop obeying his orders, preventing him from making new gains and perhaps depriving him of the old. And he had the same worries about the King of France. His doubts about the Orsinis were confirmed when, after taking Faenza, he attacked Bologna, and saw the soldiers anything but enthusiastic. Louis's position became clear when, having taken Urbino, Borgia advanced towards Tuscany only to have the French king insist he turn back. After that he decided never to rely on other people's armies and authority again.

So first of all he weakened the Orsini and Colonna factions in Rome by luring the noblemen who supported them over to his side with generous salaries and military and political appointments in line with each man's rank. In a few months old loyalties were forgotten and they were all for the duke. Then, having broken up the Colonna leaders, he waited for a

chance to eliminate the main Orsini men. The chance came
and he took it. Having realized, too late, that the growing
power of Borgia and the Church would be their ruin, the
Orsini arranged to meet together at Magione, near Perugia.
The meeting produced a rebellion in Urbino, uprisings in
Romagna and all kinds of dangers for Borgia. But with the
help of the French he won through.

Having recovered credibility, and not wanting to have to
put the loyalty of the French or anyone else to the test, Borgia
turned to trickery. He was so good at disguising his intentions
that even the Orsini made peace with him, sending Paulo
Orsini as mediator. Borgia was extremely generous to Paulo,
reassuring him with gifts of money, clothes and horses, until
the ingenuous Orsinis eventually responded and accepted an
invitation to Senigallia, thus delivering themselves into the
duke's hands. Having killed the Orsini leaders then and forced
their followers to become his allies, Borgia had laid solid
foundations for his power: he held Romagna and the Duchy
of Urbino and, what's more, he felt he had won the support of
the local people who were beginning to enjoy some prosperity.

Since this last achievement deserves to be more widely
known and imitated, I want to give it the proper space. On
taking control of Romagna, Borgia found it had been run by
weak leaders who had been stripping the people of their
wealth rather than governing them, and provoking division
rather than unity, with the result that theft, feuds and all
kinds of injustice were endemic. So he decided some good
government was required to pacify the area and force people
to respect authority. With this in mind, he appointed Remirro
de Orco, a cruel, no-nonsense man, and gave him complete
control. In a short while de Orco pacified and united the
area, establishing a considerable reputation for himself in the
process. At this point the duke decided that such draconian
powers were no longer necessary and might cause resentment.
So he set up a civil court of law in the middle of the territory

to which every town was to send a representative and he placed a distinguished man in charge. And since he was aware that the recent severity had led some people to hate him, in order to have them change their minds, and hence win them over entirely to his side, he decided to show that if the regime had been cruel, that was due to the brutal nature of his minister, not to him. So as soon as he found a pretext, he had de Orco beheaded and his corpse put on display one morning in the piazza in Cesena with a wooden block and a bloody knife beside. The ferocity of the spectacle left people both gratified and shocked.

But let's get back to where we left off. Borgia had consolidated his power and secured himself against most immediate dangers, building up an army of his own and seeing off the majority of the other armies that had been near enough to attack him. At this point the only obstacle to further expansion was the King of France. Borgia knew the king had realized he'd made a mistake supporting him earlier on and hence would not put up with further adventures. So he began to look around for new alliances and was less than generous in his support when Louis marched south to fight the Spanish who were besieging Gaeta in the northern part of the Kingdom of Naples. His aim was to be safe from French interference, something he would have managed soon enough no doubt, if his father, Pope Alexander, had not died.

So that was how Borgia dealt with the immediate situation.

As far as the future was concerned, what worried the duke most of all was that his father's eventual successor would be hostile and try to deprive him of the territory Pope Alexander had given him. He devised four strategies to guard against this: first, eliminate the families of all the local rulers whose land he had taken, thus denying a new pope the option of restoring them; second, win the support of all the noble families of Rome (as we've already seen) so as to put the brakes on any papal initiative; third, get as much control as possible of the College that would elect the next pope; fourth, win so much territory before the pope died as to be able to resist a first attack with his own resources. By the time his father died he had achieved three of these four goals and wasn't far off achieving the fourth. He had killed all the local rulers he could get his hands on and hardly anyone had escaped; he had won over the Roman nobility and he had enormous influence over the Electoral College. As far as extending his territory was concerned, he was aiming to become master of all Tuscany, having already captured Perugia and Piombino and taken Pisa under his protection.

As soon as France's restraining influence weakened (actually, it already had, since, having lost the Kingdom of Naples to Spain, the French – and the Spanish too for that matter – now needed Borgia's support) he would grab Pisa. At that point Lucca and Siena would quickly surrender, partly out of fear and partly thanks to their old enmity with Florence, after which the Florentines would be unable to defend themselves. If Borgia had managed all this (and he was almost there the very year Alexander died) he would have accumulated so much power and prestige that he could have responded to any aggression with his own forces and talent and wouldn't have needed to rely on anyone else's armies or authority. But Alexander died just five years after his son had first drawn his sword. Only in Romagna had Borgia consolidated his power; all his other territorial gains were still shaky. He was isolated, caught between two extremely powerful, hostile armies, and, what's more, mortally ill.

Borgia was so ruthless and so talented, he knew so well that you have to win over people or destroy them and he had built up such solid foundations for his power in such a short time that if he hadn't had these two armies threatening him, or if he hadn't been so ill, he would have overcome every obstacle. That the foundations Borgia had built were sound was soon evident: Romagna waited loyally for more than a month while he lay half dead in Rome, and in Rome itself no one took advantage of his weakness; when his enemies, the Baglionis, Vitellis and Orsinis, turned up no one went over to their side. And though Borgia wasn't able to choose who would be the new pope, at least he was in a position to block anyone he didn't want. So if he had been in good health when his father died, everything would have been easy. He himself told me, in the days when the College was meeting to elect Julius II, that he had thought over what might happen on his father's death and had made plans for every contingency; it was just that it never occurred to him that when the time came he too might be at death's door.

Having given this summary of everything Cesare Borgia did, I can't find anything to criticize; on the contrary, and as I said, I mean to propose him as a model for anyone who comes to power through fortunate circumstances or with the help of another ruler's armed forces. Given his great determination and considerable ambitions, Borgia could hardly have behaved any differently; only the combination of Alexander's early death and his own illness prevented him from achieving his goals. A new ruler who reckons he must ward off enemies and woo friends, overcome obstacles by force or fraud, have himself loved and feared by his people, followed and respected by his soldiers, who must eliminate enemies likely or certain to attack him, reform old institutions, show himself both severe and gracious, generous and spontaneous, break up a disloyal army and build a new one, keep the friendship of kings and princes so that they support him with deference, or at least think twice before harming him, will find no better recent example to study than the policies of Cesare Borgia.

The only criticism one can level at him is his role in the election of Pope Julius. As we've said, Borgia wasn't in a position to impose the pope he wanted but he did have influence enough to keep out the candidates he didn't want. And he should never have allowed a cardinal whose interests he had damaged, or who as pope would have reason to fear him, to win the election. Because it's fear or hatred that makes men attack each other. The cardinals Borgia had wronged were, among others, Giuliano della Rovere, cardinal of San Pietro ad Vincula, Cardinal Colonna, cardinal of San Giorgio of Savona, and Ascanio Sforza. All the others, with the exception of the cardinal of Rouen and the Spanish cardinals, would have had reason to fear him had they become pope. With the King of France behind him, the cardinal of Rouen was a very powerful man, while the Spanish cardinals were related to Borgia and indebted to him. So the best solution for Borgia was a Spanish pope; failing that, he should have let Rouen take the throne, but not Giuliano della Rovere. Anyone who thinks that an important man will forget past grievances just because he's received some new promotion must think again. Borgia miscalculated in this election, and the mistake was fatal.

8

States won by crime

Aside from lucky circumstances and positive qualities, there are two other ways a private citizen can become a ruler and we should include them in our discussion, though one of these would find more space in a book about republics. They are, first, when a man seizes power by some terrible crime and, second, when a private citizen becomes hereditary ruler with the support of his fellow citizens. As for achieving kingship by crime, we'll discuss two examples, one from ancient history and one from modern times, and look no deeper into the question, since these will be models enough for anyone obliged to take this course.

Agathocles was a Sicilian. From being a private citizen, one of the lowest of the low in fact, he became King of Syracuse. Born a potter's son, he lived a life of depravity from start to finish. All the same, mixed with that depravity were such excellent mental and physical qualities that, having joined the Syracusan army, he rose through the ranks and eventually became commander-in-chief. Once he'd taken charge, Agathocles decided to make himself king, using whatever violence was necessary to keep the power conferred on him as commander without being obliged to anyone. He discussed his intentions with Hamilcar, a Carthaginian whose army was then fighting in Sicily, and reached an agreement with him. Then one morning he called an assembly of the people and the Senate as if he had important state business to discuss.

At a prearranged signal his soldiers moved in and killed all the senators and richest men in town. After this massacre Agathocles became King of Syracuse and held his throne without any resistance from the people. Twice defeated by the Carthaginians and then actually besieged, not only did he manage to defend his town but, leaving some men behind to resist the siege, he led the rest out of Syracuse to attack Africa. The siege was lifted and the Carthaginians pushed to the brink of collapse, at which point they accepted an agreement which allowed them to keep Africa and left Sicily to Agathocles.

Looking at Agathocles' life and achievements, you won't find much that can be attributed to luck. As I said, he had no backers or benefactors when he took power but rose through the ranks, surviving all kinds of hardships and dangers. And when he'd got power he knew how to take tough, dangerous decisions to hold on to it. On the other hand, we can hardly describe killing fellow citizens, betraying friends and living without loyalty, mercy or creed as signs of talent. Methods like that may bring you power, but not glory. If you consider Agathocles' ability to take risks and come out on top, and his remarkable spirit when it came to facing and overcoming obstacles, it's hard to see why he isn't rated as highly as the most outstanding military leaders. But his brutality, cruelty and inhumanity, together with the endless crimes he committed, mean he has no place among the men we most admire. In conclusion, we can't attribute Agathocles' achievements to luck or to positive qualities, since he needed neither.

In our own times, we have the example of Oliverotto, a man from the town of Fermo who lived during the papacy of Alexander VI. Orphaned of his father while still very young, Oliverotto was brought up by his uncle, Giovanni Fogliani, who had him join the army under Paulo Vitelli in the hope that, with military discipline, he would rise to a high rank. On Paulo's death, Oliverotto served under his brother, Vitellozzo, and being very capable, with a strong personality and power-

ful physique, he soon became the army's top man. But since
he felt that working with others was demeaning, he decided
to take Fermo for himself. Having got the support of some of
the town's citizens, people who preferred to see their city
enslaved rather than free, and with the backing of Vitellozzo,
he wrote to Giovanni Fogliani saying that now so many years
had gone by he was eager to come home and see his uncle
again, visit the town, and check over some of his property.
And since, he wrote, he'd been working hard for nothing but
the prestige of his position, he wanted to ride into town in
style with a hundred mounted friends and servants beside
him; that way his fellow citizens would see that he hadn't been
wasting his time. And he asked his uncle please to arrange for
the people of Fermo to organize an appropriate reception,
something that would not only honour him but also his uncle,
who had brought him up.

Giovanni spared no effort to do his nephew proud and,
after the people of Fermo had given him a formal reception,
Oliverotto was welcomed into his uncle's house. A few days
later, having used the time to make secret arrangements for
the crime he was planning, he threw an impressive banquet
to which he invited Giovanni Fogliani and all the town's
leading men. After they'd finished eating and sat through all
the entertainments you get on these occasions, Oliverotto
slyly launched into some weighty reflections on the power
and achievements of Pope Alexander and his son Cesare
Borgia. When Giovanni and the others joined the conversation, Oliverotto suddenly got to his feet and said these were
matters best discussed in a more private place and he headed
for another room with Giovanni and all the other citizens
trailing after him. They had barely sat down before
Oliverotto's soldiers rushed out of their hiding places and
killed the lot of them.

After the massacre, Oliverotto got on his horse, rode round
the town and surrounded the chief magistrate in the state

palace, with the result that people were forced to do what he said and set up a government with Oliverotto as the ruler. Having killed everyone who opposed the coup and might hit back, he strengthened his position by setting up a new army and new civil institutions, so that within the year he was not only undisputed master of Fermo but also a serious threat to the neighbouring towns. And as with Agathocles, it would have been very hard to unseat Oliverotto, had he not let himself be fooled by Cesare Borgia, when, as explained earlier on, Borgia lured the Orsini and Vitelli men to Senigallia. Oliverotto went with them and so, just a year after killing his uncle, he was strangled along with Vitellozzo Vitelli, his mentor in courage and crime.

You might well wonder how on earth, after all their count-less betrayals and cruelties, men like Agathocles could sit safe on their thrones for years and even defend themselves against foreign enemies without their citizens ever conspiring against them; and this while many others, equally ready to use cruelty, weren't even able to hold on to their power in peacetime, never mind in war. I think it's a question of whether cruelty is well or badly used. Cruelty well used (if we can ever speak well of something bad) is short-lived and decisive, no more than is necessary to secure your position and then stop; you don't go on being cruel but use the power it has given you to deliver maximum benefits to your subjects. Cruelty is badly used when you're not drastic enough at the beginning but grow increasingly cruel later on, rather than easing off. A leader who takes the first approach has a chance, like Aga-thocles, of improving his position with his subjects and with God too; go the other way and you have no chance at all.

It's worth noting that when you take hold of a state, you must assess how much violence and cruelty will be necessary and get it over with at once, so as not to have to be cruel on a regular basis. When you've stopped using violence your subjects will be reassured and you can then win them over with generosity. If you don't do all it takes at the beginning, because you were badly advised or didn't have the nerve, then you'll always have to be wielding the knife; and you'll never be able to count on your subjects, since with all the violence you're handing out they won't be able to count on you. So get the violence over with as soon as possible; that way there'll be less time for people to taste its bitterness and they'll be less hostile. Favours, on the other hand, should be given out slowly, one by one, so that they can be properly savoured. Most of all, though, a ruler should have the kind of relationship with his subjects where nothing that can happen, good or bad, will force him to change his approach, because if hard times demand it, your cruelty will come too late, while any concessions you make will be seen as wrung out of you and no one will be impressed.

9

Monarchy with public support

Now let's turn to our second case, where a private citizen becomes king in his own country not by crime or unacceptable violence, but with the support of his fellow-citizens. We can call this a monarchy with public support and to become its king you don't have to be wholly brilliant or extraordinarily lucky, just shrewd in a lucky way. Obviously, to take control of this kind of state you need the support of either the common people or the wealthy families, the nobles. In every city one finds these two conflicting political positions: there are the common people who are eager not to be ordered around and oppressed by the noble families, and there are the nobles who are eager to oppress the common people and order them around. These opposing impulses will lead to one of three different situations: a monarchy, a republic, or anarchy.

A monarchy can be brought about either by the common people or the nobles, when one or the other party finds it convenient. Seeing that they can't control the people, the wealthy families begin to concentrate prestige on one of their number and make him king so as to be able to get what they want in his shadow. Likewise, the people, seeing that they can't resist the power of the nobles, concentrate prestige on one citizen and make him king so that his authority will protect them. A king who comes to power with the help of the rich nobles will have more trouble keeping it than the king who gets there with the support of the people, because he will be surrounded by men who consider themselves his equals, and that will make it hard for him to give them orders or to manage affairs as he wants.

But a man coming to power with the support of the common people holds it alone and has no one, or hardly anyone, around him who's unwilling to obey. What's more, you can't in good faith give the nobles what they want without doing harm to others; but you can with the people. Because the people's aspirations are more honourable than those of the nobles: the nobles want to oppress the people, while the people want to be free from oppression. What's more, a king can never be safe if the common people are hostile to him, because there are so many of them; but he can protect himself against the nobles, since there are not so many. The worst a king can expect if the people turn hostile is that they will desert him; but when the nobles turn against him, he has to fear not only desertion, but a direct attack. The nobles are smarter, they see further ahead, they always move early enough to save their skins, ingratiating themselves with whoever they think will turn out the winner. Then, of necessity, a king will always have to live with the same common people; but he can perfectly well get by without the same nobles, since he can make and unmake noblemen every day, giving and taking away honours as he likes.

Let's settle this question of the nobles. As I see it, they can be divided for the most part into two categories: either they behave in such a way as to tie themselves entirely to your destiny, or they don't. Those who do tie themselves and aren't greedy should be honoured and loved; the ones who don't can be further divided into two groups. Maybe they are anxious men, naturally lacking in character, in which case you'd better make use of them, especially the ones with good advice to offer, since when things are going well they'll respect you and when things are tough you needn't fear them; but if they're hanging back out of calculation and ambition that's a sign they're looking more to their own interests than to yours. These are the ones you have to watch out for and guard against as if they were already declared enemies, because, inevitably, when things start going wrong, these men will be working to bring you down.

A man who becomes king with the support of the people, then, must keep those people on his side. This is easy enough since all they want is to be free from oppression. But the man who becomes king against the will of the majority and with the support of the wealthy nobles must make it an absolute priority to win over the affection of the common people. This will be easy if he takes them under his protection. When people are treated well by someone they thought was hostile they respond with even greater loyalty; they'll go over to his side at once and be even more devoted than if he had taken power with their support. There are all kinds of ways a king can win the people's affection, but since these depend on particular circumstances and one can hardly lay down rules, I'll leave them out of our discussion. I'll just conclude, then, that a ruler must have the people on his side; otherwise when things get tough there'll be no way out.

Nabis, the Spartan king, was besieged by forces from all over Greece plus a hugely successful Roman army, but he held out and defended his country and his position against the lot of them. All he had to do when danger threatened was take precautions to deal with a few internal enemies, but if he'd had the people against him, this wouldn't have been enough. And if anyone objects to my reasoning here with that trite proverb: the man who builds his house on the people is building on mud, my answer is that this is true if it's a private citizen doing the building and imagining the people will come to his rescue when he's in trouble with the law or his enemies. Men like this usually find themselves being let down, as did the Gracchi brothers in Rome and Giorgio Scali in Florence. But when it's a king building on the people, and when he's a man of spirit who knows how to lead and doesn't panic when things get tough, a man who takes the right precautions and whose personality and style of government keeps everybody in a positive state of mind, then the people will never let him down and time will show what solid foundations he laid.

This kind of ruler is most at risk when passing from publicly supported leadership to absolute rule. At this point he either commands directly himself or gives orders by proxy through magistrates. If he's ruling by proxy he'll be weaker and exposed to greater risks, since he now depends entirely on the good will of the men appointed as magistrates and they can very easily strip him of his power, particularly when times are hard, either by attacking him directly or by just not carrying out his orders. Once the trouble has begun, the ruler won't have time to take absolute command himself because his citizens and subjects will be used to taking orders from magistrates and they aren't going to start obeying him in a moment of crisis; so when he's up against it, he'll always be struggling to find anyone he can trust. A ruler in this position mustn't count on what he sees when things are going well and the citizens need his government. Then everybody comes running, everyone is promising this and that, everyone is ready to die for him, since there is no question of dying. But when things get tough and it's the government that needs the citizens, then hardly anyone shows. And what's so dangerous about a critical moment like this is that you only get one shot at it. So if he's sensible the ruler must work out a situation where his citizens will always need both his government and him, however well or badly things are going. Then they will always be loyal.

10

Assessing a state's strength

When looking at the nature of these various states one important question to ask is: if attacked, does a ruler have sufficient power to defend himself with his own resources, or will he always have to rely on the protection of others? To make the question more precise, let's say that a ruler who has enough men or enough money to put together an army that can take on all comers is, by my definition, capable of defending himself, while a ruler who can't take on an enemy in the field but has to withdraw behind his city walls and defend those, is one who will always be in need of outside help. We've already said something about the first kind of ruler [Chapter 6] and later on there'll be more [Chapters 11–13]. As for the second kind, one can only encourage them to fortify their home towns and keep them well supplied, while leaving the surrounding countryside entirely to its fate. If a ruler has built good fortifications and managed his relationship with his subjects as suggested above and further elaborated in the following pages, his enemies will always think twice before attacking him. People are always wary of projects that present obvious difficulties, and attacking a well-defended town and a ruler whose subjects don't hate him is never an easy proposition.

German cities are completely independent, don't have much territory around them and obey the emperor only when it suits. They are not afraid of him, nor of any other powerful rulers in the area. This is because these towns are so well fortified that everyone realizes what an arduous, wearisome business it would be to attack them. They all have properly sized moats and walls; they have the necessary artillery; they have public warehouses with food, drink and firewood for a year; what's more, to keep people well fed without draining the public purse, they stock materials for a year's worth of work in whatever trades are the lifeblood of the city and whatever jobs the common folk earn their keep with. They hold military exercises in high regard and make all kinds of arrangements to make sure they're routinely practised.

So, a ruler whose city is well fortified and who doesn't inspire hatred among his subjects isn't going to be attacked, and even if he is, his attackers will leave humiliated, because the world is such a changeable place that it's almost impossible to keep an army camped outside a city's walls doing nothing for a whole year. Someone will object: what if people have houses outside the walls and see them being burned down; won't they get impatient; won't the long siege and their worries for their own futures make them forget their ruler? My answer is that a leader with power and personality will always get round problems like this; he can raise hopes that the siege won't last long; he can frighten people with stories about the enemy's cruelty; he can move quickly to block anyone who seems too hot-headed. Aside from this, it's obvious that the enemy is going to be burning and razing the countryside as he approaches the town at a time when people are still enthusiastic and determined to resist. This actually gives the ruler less cause for concern, because a few days later, when hearts are cooling, the damage is already done, the blow struck, and there's no way back. As a result, people will rally round their ruler all the more, they'll see him as indebted to them because their houses have been burned and their property destroyed in his defence. It's human nature to tie yourself to a leader as much for the services you've done him as the good he's done you. Hence, when you think about it, if the ruler is sensible, it won't be that hard to keep people solid throughout the siege, so long as they have food to eat and weapons to defend themselves.

II

Church states

The last kind of state we have to look at is the Church state. In this case all the difficulties an eventual ruler must face come before he takes power; because while you need ability or luck to take a state like this you can hold on to it without either. Church states are upheld by ancient religious institutions that are so strong and well established as to keep their rulers in power no matter what they do or how they live. Only Church leaders possess states without defending them and subjects without governing them. And even when undefended their states are not taken off them; even when left ungoverned their subjects don't rebel; they don't think about changing ruler and wouldn't be able to anyway. So this is the only form of government that is secure and relaxed.

But since Church states depend on forces beyond the reach of human reason, I shall say no more about them. God created them and sustains them and it would be rash and presumptuous for a mere man to discuss them. All the same, if someone were to ask me how the Church has increased its temporal power so dramatically in recent times, progressing from a situation prior to Pope Alexander where even the most insignificant rulers of Italy hardly rated the Church at all in temporal terms to one where a pope can scare the King of France himself and chase him out of Italy and crush the Venetians, then I think it would be worthwhile sorting out the facts for the record, however well known they may already be.

Before Charles, King of France, came down into Italy, the country was controlled by the pope, the Venetians, the King of Naples, the Duke of Milan and the Florentines. Necessarily, these powerful states had two main concerns: to keep foreign armies out of Italy and to prevent each other from grabbing more territory. The pope and the Venetians were the most eager expansionists. The only way to hold back the Venetians was for all the other states to band together, as they did in the defence of Ferrara; to frustrate the pope, on the other hand, they relied on the Roman barons. Since these barons were divided into two factions, the Orsinis and the Colonnas, they always had something to fight about, and with their swords drawn under the pope's nose they kept him weak and indecisive. And though from time to time you might get a really determined pope, like Sixtus, all the same he was never quite cunning enough or lucky enough to solve the problem. The reason was that papacies tended to be short-lived. In the ten years, on average, that a pope was in power he might just manage to beat down one of the two factions; but if, for example, one pope had almost finished off the Colonnas, the next would be hostile to the Orsinis and so resurrect the Colonnas, but without quite having the time to see off the Orsinis. This is why the Italian states did not rate the pope's temporal power very highly.

Then came Alexander VI, who more than any other pope in history showed what could be done with finance and force of arms. Using Valentino Borgia and taking advantage of the intrusions of the French, he made all the gains I mentioned in my discussion of Duke Valentino. And though Alexander's aim was to make his son great, not the Church, all the same his achievements enhanced the power of the Church, which, after his and then Valentino's death, inherited his conquests. So on his election Pope Julius took over a Church that now possessed the whole of Romagna and was all the more power-ful because Alexander had quashed the Roman barons and their factions. He also found a new way of increasing Church income which had never been used before.*

Julius not only followed Alexander's lead, but went further. He aimed to take Bologna, defeat the Venetians and push the French out of Italy. In the end all three goals were achieved and Julius's credit was the greater because he did it for the glory of the Church, not out of private interest. He kept the Orsini and Colonna factions in the same reduced state he found them in, and, though one or two of their leaders tried to change things, two obstacles held them back: the first was the Church's power, which unnerved them, and the second was the fact that they had no cardinals. Cardinals are always a cause of internal division; when they have their own cardinals, these factions are never quiet, because the cardinals feed party animosity both inside and outside Rome and the barons are forced to come to their party's defence. So it's the ambition of the cardinals that prompts hostility and conflict between the barons. On Julius's death, his Holiness Pope Leo found the papacy in an extremely strong position and it is to be hoped that while his predecessors made the Church great by armed force, he can make it even greater and more praiseworthy thanks to his goodness and many, many other virtues.

* The sale of Church benefices and indulgences.

12

Different kinds of armies and a consideration of mercenary forces

Now that I've given a detailed account of the characteristics of the states I set out to talk about, and examined to some extent the reasons for their being powerful or weak and the ways people in the past have tried to take and to hold them, I shall offer a more general discussion of the means of attack and defence available to each kind of state. We've already said that a ruler's power must be based on solid foundations; otherwise he's bound to fall. And the main foundations of any state, whether it be new, or old, or a new territory acquired by an old regime, are good laws and good armed forces. And since you can't have good laws if you don't have good armed forces, while if you have good armed forces good laws inevitably follow, I'll leave aside a discussion of the law and go straight to the question of the army.

Now, the armies a ruler is depending on to defend his state will either be his own, or mercenaries, or auxiliaries, or some combination of these. Mercenaries and auxiliaries are useless and dangerous. If you are counting on mercenaries to defend your state you will never be stable or secure, because mercenaries are ambitious, undisciplined, disloyal and they quarrel among themselves. Courageous with friends and cowardly with enemies, they have no fear of God and keep no promises. With mercenaries the only way to delay disaster is to delay the battle; in peacetime they plunder you and in wartime they let the enemy plunder you. Why? Because the only interest they have in you and their only reason for fighting is the meagre salary you're paying them, and that's not reason enough to make them want to die for you. Sure, they're happy to be your soldiers while you're not at war, but when war comes, they run for it, or just disappear.

It shouldn't be hard to convince the reader of this, since Italy's present ruin has been caused precisely by a prolonged dependence on mercenaries. It's true that mercenary forces did win some battles and seemed courageous when fighting other mercenaries; but as soon as a foreign army turned up we saw what they were made of: Charles, King of France, didn't even have to fight; his men just put chalk crosses on the buildings they planned to use as billets. When Savonarola said we brought this on ourselves with our own sins, he was right; except the sins were not what he was thinking of, but the ones I've been talking about. And because they were our rulers' sins, it was our rulers who paid the price.

I'd like to offer a better explanation of why mercenaries are not a good idea. A mercenary commander may or may not be an excellent military leader: if he is, you can't trust him because he will always aspire to power himself, either by attacking you, his paymaster, or by attacking others against your wishes; but if he isn't a capable leader, he'll ruin you anyway. And if someone objects that it hardly matters who commands the army since commanders always behave like this, whether mercenary or no, my response is as follows: armed forces are always at the service of a hereditary ruler or a republic. A ruler must go in person and act as commander himself; a republic must send its citizens; if it sends a man who turns out to be no good it must replace him; if he is good it must keep him in line with laws that prevent him exceeding his brief. Experience shows that only rulers and republics with their own armies make serious progress, while mercenaries bring nothing but trouble. And a republic with a citizen army is less likely to fall victim to a coup than a republic paying for mercenary armies.

Rome and Sparta stood for many centuries armed and free. The Swiss are extremely well armed and completely free. One example of the use of mercenaries in ancient times is Carthage. After the first war with Rome the Carthaginians were almost overthrown by their mercenaries despite the fact that these men were commanded by Carthaginian citizens. After the death of Epaminondas the Thebans made Philip of Macedonia commander of their army and no sooner had he won the war than he stripped them of their freedom. On the death of Filippo Maria Visconti, the Milanese hired Francesco Sforza to fight against the Venetians. Having beaten the Venetians at Caravaggio, Sforza joined forces with them to overthrow his paymasters, the Milanese. When Francesco's father was mercenary commander for Queen Joanna of Naples, he suddenly made off and left her undefended so that she had to put herself into the hands of the King of Aragon or risk losing her kingdom.

It's true that in the past both Venice and Florence did increase their territories with the use of mercenaries whose commanders did not seize power but actually defended their employers. The fact is that the Florentines were lucky; various powerful captains were indeed potential threats, but one didn't win his war, while others either found themselves facing strong opposition or turned their ambitions elsewhere. The one who didn't win was Giovanni Acuto [John Hawkwood], and since he lost we don't know whether he would have been loyal or not; but everyone must admit that, had he won, the Florentines would have been at his mercy. Francesco Sforza had the forces of Braccio da Montone against him and the two commanders kept each other in check: Sforza turned his ambitions to Lombardy while Braccio went to fight Rome and Naples.

But let's remember what happened just a short while ago. Florence took on Paulo Vitelli as military commander, an extremely serious man who had come from nothing to achieve enormous prestige. Had he taken Pisa for them, you could hardly deny that the Florentines would have been right to hang on to him, because if he had gone over to the enemy, they wouldn't have had a chance; but keeping him would have meant accepting him as their ruler.

Turning to the Venetians, we find they fought confidently and successfully when they fought for themselves, at sea that is, where both nobles and armed commoners showed great courage. But when they began to fight on land, they left these strengths behind and, like other Italian states, hired mercenaries. In the early stages of their expansion on the mainland they had so little territory and so much prestige they hardly needed to worry about their mercenary commanders; but when they pushed deeper into the peninsula, under the leadership of Carmagnola, they got a taste of the trouble mercenaries bring. They'd seen what a fine commander Carmagnola was and under his leadership they had defeated the Duke of Milan, so they soon noticed when he lost his enthusiasm for the war. They realized they couldn't win anything else with him, because that wasn't what he wanted, but they couldn't fire him either for fear of losing what they had previously won; at which point the only safe thing to do was to kill him. Later they hired Bartolomeo da Bergamo, Ruberto da San Severino, Niccolò Orsini, Count of Pitigliano, and other such mercenary commanders who were always more likely to lose than win, and in fact at the battle of Vailà the Venetians eventually lost in a single day all the gains they had so determinedly accumulated over the past 800 years. The fact is that mercenaries bring only slow, belated, unconvincing victories, then sudden, bewildering defeats. Since these examples all have to do with Italy, which has been dominated by mercenaries for many years, I'd now like to get a broader view of the problem, because if we can trace its origin and developments it will be easier to find a solution.

What we must remember is that over recent centuries, as

the empire began to lose its hold in Italy while the pope increased his temporal power, so the country broke up into smaller states. Many of the larger cities rose up against the local nobles who had needed the emperor's backing to keep control of them; the Church supported the rebels to increase its own political influence. In many other towns private citizens took over as rulers. The result was that with much of Italy now controlled by the Church and republics, which is to say by people who had no experience of war, leaders began to hire men from outside. The first successful mercenary commander was Alberigo da Conio from Romagna. With what they learned from him, Braccio da Montone and Francesco Sforza and others would become arbiters of Italy's destiny. After them came all the other mercenary commanders down to our own times. And the end result of all their genius is that Italy was overrun by Charles, ransacked by Louis, torn apart by Ferdinand and humiliated by the Swiss.

The mercenaries' first tactic was to increase their own importance by playing down the importance of infantry. Having no territory of their own and living on what they got from fighting, they couldn't feed large numbers of infantry, while smaller numbers weren't sufficiently impressive; so they concentrated on cavalry and were fed and respected with more manageable numbers. Things reached the point where an army of 20,000 would have fewer than 2,000 infantry. Aside from this the mercenaries did everything possible to avoid hard work and danger; they wouldn't kill each other in combat but took prisoners, then didn't even ask for a ransom. They wouldn't attack fortifications at night; and they wouldn't leave their own fortifications to attack a besieging army's camp. They didn't dig ditches or build stockades round their camps; in winter they didn't camp out at all. All these omissions became accepted practice for the simple reason, as I said, that they wanted to steer clear of danger and hard work. Thus they brought Italy to slavery and humiliation.

13

Auxiliaries, combined forces and citizen armies

Auxiliary armies – that is, when you ask a powerful ruler to send military help to defend your town – are likewise useless. In recent times we have the example of Pope Julius during his Ferrara campaign: having seen what a sad lot his mercenaries were in battle, he reached an agreement with Ferdinand, King of Spain, to have his forces come to help. Auxiliaries may be efficient and useful when it comes to achieving their own ends, but they are almost always counterproductive for those who invite them in, because if they lose, you lose too, and if they win, you are at their mercy.

Although ancient history is full of pertinent examples, I'd like to stick to this recent case of Pope Julius II, whose decision to put himself entirely in a foreign army's hands merely to take Ferrara could hardly have been more rash. But he was lucky and the unlikely outcome of the campaign spared him the possible consequences of his mistake: when his Spanish auxiliaries were beaten at Ravenna, the Swiss turned up and against all expectations – the pope's included – routed the hitherto victorious French, so that Julius escaped being a prisoner either to his enemies, who had fled, or to his auxiliaries, who weren't the ones to win the day for him. The Florentines, who had no armed forces at all, took 10,000 French auxiliaries to lay siege to Pisa, a decision that put them in greater danger than any they had experienced in their whole troubled history. To fight his neighbours, the emperor of

Constantinople brought 10,000 Turks into Greece and when the war was over they wouldn't leave, which was how the infidels began to get control of Greece.

So anyone looking for a no-win situation should turn to auxiliaries, because they are far more dangerous even than mercenaries. With auxiliaries your ruin is guaranteed: they are a tightly knit force and every one of them obedient to someone else; when mercenaries win they need time and a convenient opportunity before they can attack you, if only because they're not a solid united force, you chose them, you're paying them, and hence it will take the man you put in command a while to build up sufficient authority to turn against you. To summarize, the big danger with mercenaries is their indecision, with auxiliaries their determination.

So, sensible rulers have always avoided using auxiliaries and mercenaries, relying instead on their own men and even preferring to lose with their own troops than to win with others, on the principle that a victory won with foreign forces is not a real victory at all. As always Cesare Borgia offers a good example. He invaded Romagna with an army entirely made up of French auxiliaries and took Imola and Forlì with them; but since he felt they weren't reliable he turned to mercenaries as a less dangerous option. He hired the Orsini and Vitelli armies, but when he found that they dithered in battle and were disloyal and dangerous, he had them killed and trained his own men. It's easy to see the difference between these various kinds of armies if you look at the duke's standing when he had just the French, when he had the Orsinis and the Vitellis, and when he had his own soldiers and relied on his own resources. With each change his prestige grew and he was only truly respected when everyone could see that his troops were entirely his own.

I had planned to stick to these recent Italian examples, but I wouldn't like to leave out Hiero of Syracuse since he is one of the men I talked about before. Given command, as I explained, of the Syracusan armies, Hiero soon realized that the mercenaries among them were no good, led as they were by men like our Italian commanders. Realizing that he could neither make use of them nor let them go, he had them all cut to pieces, and from then on fought only with his own soldiers. I'd also like to bring in a parable from the Old Testament. When David offered to go and fight the Philistine trouble-maker, Goliath, on Saul's behalf, Saul gave him his own weapons to bolster the boy's courage. But no sooner had David put them on than he refused the gift, saying he wouldn't feel confident with them, he would rather face the enemy with his own sling and knife. In the end, other people's arms are either too loose, too heavy or too tight.

When, with luck and good leadership, Charles VII, Louis XI's father, had pushed the English out of France, he saw that a ruler needs his own troops and so set up a standing army of both cavalry and infantry. Later, his son Louis disbanded the infantry and began to hire Swiss mercenaries. It's now plain that this mistake, together with others that followed, is what lies behind France's present troubles. By giving this important role to the Swiss, Louis had weakened his whole army, since, with no infantry of their own, his cavalry were now relying on others, and once they'd got used to fighting alongside the Swiss they started to think they couldn't win without them. As a result the French are unable to take on the Swiss in battle and won't fight anyone else without their help. So French forces are now mixed, part mercenary and part their own men. Such composite forces are much better than just auxiliaries or just mercenaries, but much worse than having all your own men. France's situation proves the point, because if the standing army Charles recruited had been reinforced or just maintained, the French would be unbeatable. But men are so thoughtless they'll opt for a diet that tastes good without realizing there's a hidden poison in it: it's like the problem I mentioned earlier about people not diagnosing tuberculosis until it's too late.

So, if a man can't spot a problem in the making, he can't really be a wise leader. But very few men have this gift. If you look for the initial cause of the collapse of the Roman empire, you'll find it was when they started hiring Goths as mercenaries. From that moment on the strength of the empire began to decline and all the determination that drained out of it went to strengthen its rivals.

So, to conclude: no state is secure without its own army; if it hasn't got men to defend it determinedly and loyally in a crisis, it is simply relying on luck. As those who understand these things have always thought and said: *There is nothing so weak and unstable as a reputation for power that is not backed up by its own army.** And having your own army means having a force made up of subjects, or citizens, or men dependent on you. All other forces are mercenaries or auxiliaries. To see how to set up your own armed forces, all you need do is consider how the four men I mentioned above organized and arranged theirs, or Philip, Alexander the Great's father, or many other kingdoms and republics. They are all entirely reliable models.

---

* Quod nihil sit tam infirmum aut instabile quam fama potentiae non sua vi nixa.

14

A ruler and his army

A ruler, then, must have no other aim or consideration, nor seek to develop any other vocation outside war, the organization of the army and military discipline. This is the only proper vocation of the man in command. And it's such a potent one that it not only keeps those born to rule on their thrones but often raises private citizens to political power. Vice versa, when rulers think more about frills than fighting they lose their thrones. In fact, the thing most likely to bring about a ruler's downfall is his neglect of the art of war; the thing most likely to win him power is becoming an expert in it.

A military man with his own army, Francesco Sforza rose from commoner to Duke of Milan; shunning military hardships, his sons fell from dukes to commoners. For one of the many negative consequences of not having an army is that people will find you pathetic, and this is a stigma a ruler must guard against, as I'll explain. The fact is that between a man who has an army and a man who hasn't there is simply no comparison. And there is no reason why a man who commands an armed force should willingly obey a man who doesn't, or why a man who doesn't command an army should live safely beside a servant who does. The one will harbour contempt and the other suspicion and they won't be able to work well together. So, quite apart from the other disadvantages, a ruler who doesn't involve himself in military matters won't, as I've said, have his soldiers' respect and won't be able to trust them.

A ruler, then, must never stop thinking about war and preparing for war and he must work at it even more in peacetime than in war itself. He can do this in two ways, physically and mentally. Physically, aside from keeping his men exercised and disciplined, he should go hunting a great deal, which will toughen up his body. It will also help him get to know different landscapes, how the mountains rise and the valleys open out, the lie of the plains, what rivers and marshes are like. These are things he should study really carefully since this kind of knowledge is useful in two ways. First, he'll get to know his own country and hence will have a better sense of how it can be defended. Second, familiarity with these places will make it easier for him to grasp the topography of places he needs to understand but hasn't seen before. The hills, valleys, plains, rivers and marshes of Tuscany, for example, have much in common with those of other areas, so that knowing the lie of the land in one region makes it easier to get to know it in another. The ruler who doesn't have this facility lacks the first thing a commander needs, because understanding the land helps you find the enemy, lead your army by the right route, choose a place to camp, plan out the battle and lay siege to a town, all in the best way possible.

One of the things historians admired about the Achaean leader Philopoemen was that even in peacetime he thought of nothing but military strategy and when he was in the country with his friends he would often stop and ask them: If the enemy were over there on that hill and we were down here with our army, who would be in the better position? How could we attack them without breaking ranks? If we decided to retreat, how would we do it? And if they retreated, how would we go after them? And as he and his friends went along he would list all the predicaments an army can find itself in. He listened to their ideas, expressed and explained his own;

so much so that, thanks to this constant work of mental preparation, when he was back leading his armies there was simply nothing that could happen that he didn't know how to deal with.

Another thing a ruler must do to exercise his mind is read history, in particular accounts of great leaders and their achievements. He should look at their wartime strategies and study the reasons for their victories and defeats so as to avoid the failures and imitate the successes. Above all he must do what some great men have done in the past: take as model a leader who's been much praised and admired and keep his example and achievements in mind at all times. Alexander the Great, it seems, modelled himself on Achilles, Caesar on Alexander and Scipio on Cyrus. Anyone who reads Xenophon's life of Cyrus will see how valuable his example was to Scipio, and how closely Scipio's decency, charm, humanity and generosity conform to the description Xenophon gives of Cyrus. A sensible leader must follow this advice and never relax in peacetime but work hard to make the most of it and turn it to his advantage in the tough times ahead. That way, when his luck does turn, he'll be ready.

15

What men and particularly rulers are praised and blamed for

It's time to look at how a ruler should behave with his subjects and his friends. Given that a great deal has already been written about this, I fear people may find my contribution presumptuous, especially since, here more than elsewhere, the code of conduct I'm offering will be rather controversial. But since my aim was to write something useful for anyone interested, I felt it would be appropriate to go to the real truth of the matter, not to repeat other people's fantasies. Many writers have dreamed up republics and kingdoms that bear no resemblance to experience and never existed in reality; there is such a gap between how people actually live and how they ought to live that anyone who declines to behave as people do, in order to behave as they should, is schooling himself for catastrophe and had better forget personal security: if you always want to play the good man in a world where most people are not good, you'll end up badly. Hence, if a ruler wants to survive, he'll have to learn to stop being good, at least when the occasion demands.

So leaving aside things people have dreamed up about rulers and concentrating instead on reality, let's say that when we talk about anyone, but especially about leaders, who are more exposed than others to the public eye, what we point are the qualities that prompt praise or blame. One man is thought generous and another miserly; one is seen as benevolent, another as grasping; one cruel, the other kind; one treacherous, another loyal; one effeminate and fearful, another bold and brave; one considerate, another arrogant; one promiscuous, another chaste; one straightforward, another devious; one stubborn, another accommodating; one solemn, another superficial; one religious, another unbelieving, and so on.

And I'm sure we'd all agree that it would be an excellent thing if a ruler were to have all the good qualities mentioned above and none of the bad; but since it's in the nature of life that you can't have or practise all those qualities all of the time, a ruler must take care to avoid the disgrace that goes with the kind of failings that could lose him his position. As for failings that wouldn't lead to his losing power, he should avoid them if he can; but if he can't, he needn't worry too much. In the same way, he mustn't be concerned about the bad reputation that comes with those negative qualities that are almost essential if he is to hold on to power. If you think about it, there'll always be something that looks morally right but would actually lead a ruler to disaster, and something else that looks wrong but will bring security and success.

16

Generosity and meanness

If we take the first of the qualities listed above, we can say that it would be nice to be seen as generous. All the same, being generous just to be seen to be so will damage you. Generosity practised out of real good will, as it should be, risks passing unnoticed and you won't escape a reputation for meanness. Hence, if you're determined to have people think of you as generous, you'll have to be lavish in every possible way; naturally, a ruler who follows this policy will soon use up all his wealth to the point that, if he wants to keep up his reputation, he'll have to impose special taxes and do everything a ruler can to raise cash. His people will start to hate him and no one will respect him now he has no money. Since his generosity will have damaged the majority and bene-fited only a few, he'll be vulnerable to the first bad news, and the first real danger may well topple him. When he realizes this and tries to change his ways, he'll immediately be accused of meanness.

Since a ruler can't be generous and show it without putting himself at risk, if he's sensible he won't mind getting a repu-tation for meanness. With time, when people see that his penny-pinching means he doesn't need to raise taxes and can defend the country against attack and embark on campaigns without putting a burden on his people, he'll increasingly be seen as generous – generous to those he takes nothing from, which is to say almost everybody, and mean to those who get nothing from him, which is to say very few. In our own times the only leaders we've seen doing great things were all reckoned mean. The others were failures. Pope Julius II exploited his reputation for generosity to get the papacy, then gladly let it go to finance his wars. The present King of France has fought many wars without resorting to new taxes, something he can do because his constant cost-cutting has provided for the extra expenditure. The present King of Spain would not have won all the wars he has if he had had a reputation for generosity.

So, if as a result he has the resources to defend his country, isn't obliged to steal from his subjects or prey on others, and is in no danger of falling into poverty, a ruler need hardly worry about a reputation for meanness; it is one of the negative qualities that keep him in power. And if someone protests: But it was generosity that won Caesar the empire and many others have risen to the highest positions because they were and were seen to be generous, my response is: A ruler in power and a man seeking power are two different things. For the ruler already in power generosity is dangerous; for the man seeking power it is essential. Caesar was one of a number of men who wanted to become emperor of Rome; but if he'd survived as emperor and gone on spending in the same way, he would have destroyed the empire. And if someone were to object: Many rulers who scored great military victories were considered extremely generous, I'd reply: Either a ruler is spending his own and his subjects' money, or someone else's. When the money is his own or his subjects', he should go easy; when it's someone else's, he should be as lavish as he can.

A ruler leading his armies and living on plunder, pillage and extortion is using other people's money and had better be generous with it, otherwise his soldiers won't follow him. What's not your own or your subjects' can be given away freely: Cyrus did this; so did Caesar and Alexander. Spending other people's money doesn't lower your standing – it raises it. It's only spending your own money that puts you at risk. Nothing consumes itself so much as generosity, because while you practise it you're losing the wherewithal to go on practising it. Either you fall into poverty and are despised for it, or, to avoid poverty, you become grasping and hateful. Above all else a king must guard against being despised and hated. Generosity leads to both. It's far more sensible to keep a reputation for meanness, which carries a stigma but doesn't rouse people's hatred, than to strive to be seen as generous and find at the end of the day that you're thought of as grasping, something that carries a stigma and gets you hated too.

17

Cruelty and compassion. Whether it's better to be feared or loved

Continuing with our list of qualities, I'm sure every leader would wish to be seen as compassionate rather than cruel. All the same he must be careful not to use his compassion unwisely. Cesare Borgia was thought to be cruel, yet his cruelty restored order to Romagna and united it, making the region peaceful and loyal. When you think about it, he was much more compassionate than the Florentines whose reluctance to be thought cruel led to disaster in Pistoia. A ruler mustn't worry about being labelled cruel when it's a question of keeping his subjects loyal and united; using a little exemplary severity, he will prove more compassionate than the leader whose excessive compassion leads to public disorder, muggings and murder. That kind of trouble tends to harm everyone, while the death sentences that a ruler hands out affect only the individuals involved. But of all rulers, a man new to power simply cannot avoid a reputation for cruelty, since a newly conquered state is a very dangerous place. Virgil puts these words in Queen Dido's mouth:

The difficult situation and the newness of my kingdom
Force me to do these things, and guard my borders everywhere.*

---

* Res dura, et regni novitas me talia cogunt
Moliri, et late fines custode tueri.

All the same, a leader must think carefully before believing and responding to certain allegations and not get frightened over nothing. He should go about things coolly, cautiously and humanely: if he's too trusting, he'll get careless, and if he trusts no one he'll make himself unbearable.

These reflections prompt the question: is it better to be loved rather than feared, or vice versa? The answer is that one would prefer to be both but, since they don't go together easily, if you have to choose, it's much safer to be feared than loved. We can say this of most people: that they are ungrateful and unreliable; they lie, they fake, they're greedy for cash and they melt away in the face of danger. So long as you're generous and, as I said before, not in immediate danger, they're all on your side: they'd shed their blood for you, they'd give you their belongings, their lives, their children. But when you need them they turn their backs on you. The ruler who has relied entirely on their promises and taken no other precautions is lost. Friendship that comes at a price, and not because people admire your spirit and achievements, may indeed have been paid for, but that doesn't mean you really possess it and you certainly won't be able to count on it when you need it. Men are less worried about letting down someone who has made himself loved than someone who makes himself feared. Love binds when someone recognizes he should be grateful to you, but, since men are a sad lot, gratitude is forgotten the moment it's inconvenient. Fear means fear of punishment, and that's something people never forget.

All the same, while a ruler can't expect to inspire love when making himself feared, he must avoid arousing hatred. Actually, being feared is perfectly compatible with not being hated. And a ruler won't be hated if he keeps his hands off his subjects' property and their women. If he really has to have someone executed, he should only do it when he has proper justification and manifest cause. Above all, he mustn't seize other people's property. A man will sooner forget the death of his father than the loss of his inheritance. Of course there are always reasons for taking people's property and a ruler who has started to live that way will never be short of pretexts for grabbing more. On the other hand, reasons for executing a man come more rarely and pass more quickly.

But when a ruler is leading his army and commanding large numbers of soldiers, then above all he must have no qualms about getting a reputation for cruelty; otherwise it will be quite impossible to keep the army united and fit for combat. One of Hannibal's most admirable achievements was that despite leading a huge and decidedly multiracial army far from home there was never any dissent among the men or rebellion against their leader whether in victory or defeat. The only possible explanation for this was Hannibal's tremendous cruelty, which, together with his countless positive qualities, meant that his soldiers always looked up to him with respect and terror. The positive qualities without the cruelty wouldn't have produced the same effect. Historians are just not thinking when they praise him for this achievement and then condemn him for the cruelty that made it possible.

To show that Hannibal's other qualities wouldn't have done the job alone we can take the case of Scipio, whose army mutinied in Spain. Scipio was an extremely rare commander not only in his own times but in the whole of recorded history, but he was too easy-going and as a result gave his troops a freedom that was hardly conducive to military discipline. Fabius Maximus condemned him for this in the Senate, claiming that he had corrupted the Roman army. When one of his officers sacked the town of Locri, Scipio again showed leniency; he didn't carry out reprisals on behalf of the towns-folk and failed to punish the officer's presumption, so much so that someone defending Scipio in the Senate remarked that he was one of those many men who don't make mistakes themselves, but find it hard to punish others who do. If Scipio had gone on leading his armies like this, with time his temperament would have undermined his fame and diminished his glory, but since he took his orders from the Senate, not only was the failing covered up but it actually enhanced his reputation.

Going back, then, to the question of being feared or loved, my conclusion is that since people decide for themselves whether to love a ruler or not, while it's the ruler who decides whether they're going to fear him, a sensible man will base his power on what he controls, not on what others have freedom to choose. But he must take care, as I said, that people don't come to hate him.

18

A ruler and his promises

Everyone will appreciate how admirable it is for a ruler to keep his word and be honest rather than deceitful. However, in our own times we've had examples of leaders who've done great things without worrying too much about keeping their word. Outwitting opponents with their cunning, these men achieved more than leaders who behaved honestly.

The reader should bear in mind that there are two ways of doing battle: using the law and using force. Typically, humans use laws and animals force. But since playing by the law often proves inadequate, it makes sense to resort to force as well. Hence a ruler must be able to exploit both the man and the beast in himself to the full. In ancient times writers used fables to teach their leaders this lesson: they tell how Achilles and many other leaders were sent to the centaur Chiron to be fed and brought up under his discipline. This story of having a teacher who was half-man and half-beast obviously meant that a ruler had to be able to draw on both natures. If he had only one, he wouldn't survive.

Since a ruler has to be able to act the beast, he should take on the traits of the fox and the lion; the lion can't defend itself against snares and the fox can't defend itself from wolves. So you have to play the fox to see the snares and the lion to scare off the wolves. A ruler who just plays the lion and forgets the fox doesn't know what he's doing. Hence a sensible leader cannot and must not keep his word if by doing so he puts himself at risk, and if the reasons that made him give his word in the first place are no longer valid. If all men were good, this would be bad advice, but since they are a sad lot and won't be keeping their promises to you, you hardly need to keep yours to them. Anyway, a ruler will never be short of good reasons to explain away a broken promise. It would be easy to cite any number of examples from modern times to show just how many peace treaties and other commitments have been rendered null and void by rulers not keeping their word. Those best at playing the fox have done better than the others. But you have to know how to disguise your slyness, how to pretend one thing and cover up another. People are so gullible and so caught up with immediate concerns that a con man will always find someone ready to be conned.

There's one recent example that really should be mentioned. Pope Alexander VI never did anything but con people. That was all he ever thought about. And he always found people he could con. No one ever gave more convincing promises than Alexander, or swore greater oaths to back them up, and no one ever kept his promises less; yet his deceptions always worked, because he knew this side of human nature so well.

So, a leader doesn't have to possess all the virtuous qualities I've mentioned, but it's absolutely imperative that he seem to possess them. I'll go so far as to say this: if he had those qualities and observed them all the time, he'd be putting himself at risk. It's seeming to be virtuous that helps; as, for example, seeming to be compassionate, loyal, humane, honest and religious. And you can even be those things, so long as you're always mentally prepared to change as soon as your interests are threatened. What you have to understand is that a ruler, especially a ruler new to power, can't always behave in ways that would make people think a man good, because to stay in power he's frequently obliged to act against loyalty, against charity, against humanity and against religion. What matters is that he has the sort of character that can change tack as luck and circumstances demand, and, as I've already said, stick to the good if he can but know how to be bad when the occasion demands.

So a ruler must be extremely careful not to say anything that doesn't appear to be inspired by the five virtues listed above; he must seem and sound wholly compassionate, wholly loyal, wholly humane, wholly honest and wholly religious. There is nothing more important than appearing to be religious. In general people judge more by appearances than first-hand experience, because everyone gets to see you but hardly anyone deals with you directly. Everyone sees what you seem to be, few have experience of who you really are, and those few won't have the courage to stand up to majority opinion underwritten by the authority of state. When they're weighing up what someone has achieved – and this is particularly true with rulers, who can't be held to account – people look at the end result. So if a leader does what it takes to win power and keep it, his methods will always be reckoned honourable and widely praised. The crowd is won over by appearances and final results. And the world is all crowd: the dissenting few find no space so long as the majority have any grounds at all for their opinions. There's a certain king today* – I'd better not call him by name – who never stops preaching peace and trust and is actually sworn enemy to both; and if he had ever practised either he would have lost his authority or his kingdom many times over.

---

* Ferdinand of Aragon.

19

Avoiding contempt and hatred

Now that I've discussed the most important of the qualities I listed I'd like to look at the others more briefly in relation to the principle, already mentioned, that a ruler must avoid any behaviour that will lead to his being hated or held in contempt; every time he manages this he's done what a ruler should and can indulge other bad habits without worrying about the consequences. As I've already said, what most leads to a ruler being hated is seizing and stealing his subjects' property and women; that he must not do. As long as you don't deprive them of property or honour most men will be happy enough and you'll only have to watch out for the ambitious few who can easily be reined back in various ways. You'll be held in contempt, on the other hand, if you're seen as changeable, superficial, effeminate, fearful or indecisive. So a ruler must avoid those qualities like so many stumbling blocks and act in such a way that everything he does gives an impression of greatness, spirit, seriousness and strength; when presiding over disputes between citizens he should insist that his decision is final and make sure no one imagines they can trick or outwit him.

The ruler who projects this impression of himself will be highly thought of and it's hard to conspire against a man who is well thought of. Then so long as he has a reputation for excellence and is respected by his people it will be hard for outside enemies to attack him either. A ruler must guard against two kinds of danger: one internal, coming from his own people; the other external, coming from foreign powers. To defend yourself against foreign powers you need a good army and good allies. And if you have a good army you'll always have good allies, and when you're secure against foreign powers you'll always be secure internally too, assuming there wasn't already a conspiracy under way. Then even when a foreign power does move against you, if you've lived and organized yourself as I've suggested, you only have to keep your nerve and you'll survive any and every attack, like the Spartan ruler Nabis in the example I gave earlier.

To get back to the internal situation: when there is no threat from outside, a ruler must take care that his subjects don't start conspiring against him. He can guard against this by making sure he isn't hated or despised and that people are happy with him, all of which is very important, as I've explained at length. In fact, one of the most powerful preventive measures against conspiracies is simply not being hated by a majority of the people. People planning a conspiracy must believe that killing the ruler will be popular; when they realize that, on the contrary, it would be unpopular they lose heart, because conspiracies are always beset with endless difficulties. Experience shows that for every successful conspiracy there are any number of failures. A conspirator can't act alone and can look for accomplices only among people he believes are unhappy with the situation. But as soon as he reveals his intentions to someone else he's giving that person the chance to improve his position, since obviously there are all kinds of advantages to be had from betraying a conspiracy. When you reckon that the benefits of betrayal are assured, while joining a conspiracy is a risky and extremely dangerous business, the man will have to be a rare friend indeed, or a very bitter enemy of the government, if he's going to keep faith.

To summarize: on the conspirator's side all you have is

fear, envy and the demoralizing prospect of punishment, while the ruler on his side has the authority of the government and its laws plus the protection of his friends and the state. Add to all that the good will of the people and it's extremely unlikely that anyone will be so crazy as to start a conspiracy. Because, while in general a conspirator has most to fear prior to the coup, in this case, with the people against him, he's going to be in danger afterwards too and the fact that he's seen off the ruler doesn't mean he can expect to escape unscathed.

I could give infinite examples of this but let's make do with just one that happened in our fathers' times. Annibale Bentivogli, grandfather of the present Annibale, was Duke of Bologna when the Canneschis conspired against him and killed him. At that point the only surviving Bentivogli was his son, Giovanni, who was still a baby. All the same, immediately after the murder, the people rose up and killed all the Canneschis. This was because the Bentivogli family was extremely popular at the time. In fact, when the Bolognese realized that with Annibale dead there were no family members capable of ruling the town, they went to Florence to get a man who was supposedly a Bentivogli, though until shortly before that he had passed himself off as the son of a blacksmith; they asked him to govern Bologna and he duly did so until Giovanni was old enough to take over.

My conclusion, then, is that so long as he has the people on his side a ruler needn't worry about conspiracies, but when they are against him and hate him he'll have to watch everyone's every move. Sensible rulers and well-run states have always done all they can not to drive the nobles to despair and to keep the people happy and satisfied; indeed this is one of a ruler's most important tasks.

One of the better organized and well-governed states in our own times is France. It is full of good institutions which guarantee the king's security and freedom of action. The most important of these is parliament and parliamentary authority.

In fact the king who set up the country's constitution was aware of the ambition and presumption of the nobles and reckoned they needed a bit in their mouths to rein them back. He also knew how much the people hated and feared the nobles and he wanted to protect them. But it was important that the king shouldn't be personally responsible for doing this since then he might be blamed by the nobles for favouring the people or by the people for favouring the nobles. So he introduced an independent body, parliament, that could keep the nobles in their place and protect the people without the king's being responsible. There really couldn't be a better or more sensible institution, nor one more conducive to the security of the king and the realm. This prompts the following reflection: that a ruler must get others to carry out policies that will provoke protest, keeping those that inspire gratitude to himself. In conclusion, let me repeat that a ruler should respect the nobles but must make sure he is not hated by the people.

Perhaps many readers familiar with the fate of certain Roman emperors will feel that their examples contradict these opinions of mine, in that they consistently behaved well and showed great character but nevertheless lost their empire or even their lives at the hands of subjects who conspired against them. To meet these objections, I shall consider the qualities of some of these emperors, showing how the causes of their downfall are not at all out of line with my reasoning above, and bringing into the argument some of the context that historians of the period consider important. I hope it will be enough to take all the emperors who held power from the philosopher Marcus Aurelius down to Maximinus, which is to say: Marcus, his son Commodus, Pertinax, Julian, Severus, Antoninus Caracalla his son, Macrinus, Heliogabalus, Alexander and Maximinus.

The first thing to note is that, while in other states a ruler has only to guard against the ambition of the nobles and the disrespect of the people, Roman emperors faced a third hazard: the greed and cruelty of the army. This was such a tough problem that it proved the downfall of many emperors, because it was so hard to keep both the people and the army happy. The people were for a quiet life and hence loved low-profile leaders, while the soldiers loved leaders with military ambitions, men who were brazen, grasping and cruel; they wanted the emperor to unleash these qualities on the people so that they could double their incomes and give vent to their own greed and cruelty.

As a result, emperors who for lack of natural authority or political flair didn't have the kind of standing that could hold both soldiers and people in check always ended badly. When they saw how difficult it was to deal with these conflicting demands, most of them, and especially those new to power, chose to satisfy the army and more or less ignored the people's suffering. It was a policy dictated by necessity: if a ruler can't avoid hatred altogether, he must first try to avoid the hatred of the country as a whole, and when that proves impossible he must do everything he can to escape the hatred of the classes that wield the most power. So emperors new to their positions and in need of special support turned to the army rather than the people, a policy that worked for as long as they were able to maintain their prestige in the eyes of the soldiers.

This is why, although Marcus, Pertinax and Alexander were benign, humane men, who led unassuming lives, loving justice and hating cruelty, only Marcus managed to avoid a sad end and still commanded respect at his death. This was because he succeeded to the emperor's throne by hereditary right and owed nothing to either the soldiers or the people. Possessing many good qualities that aroused general admiration, he kept both the people and the army in their place throughout his reign and was never either hated or despised. But Pertinax was made emperor against the army's will; under

Commodus the soldiers had got used to a degenerate lifestyle and wouldn't accept the standards of honesty Pertinax tried to impose on them. This aroused their hatred and since Pertinax was also despised for being old he was soon overthrown.

In this regard it's worth noting that you can be hated just as much for the good you do as the bad, which is why, as I said before, a ruler who wants to stay in power is often forced not to be good. Because when a powerful group – whether they be the common people, the army or the nobility – is corrupt, then if you reckon you need their support you'll have to play to their mood and keep them happy, and at that point any good you do will only put you at risk. But let's move on to Alexander. He was such a good man that among the many things he was praised for was the fact that over fourteen years in power he never had anyone executed without a trial. All the same, people despised him; they thought him effeminate and said he let his mother run the show; as a result the army conspired against him and killed him.

Going to the opposite extreme and looking at the characters of Commodus, Severus, Antoninus Caracalla and Maximinus, we find they were extremely cruel and grasping; to keep the army happy they committed every crime a leader can commit against his people and all of them, with the exception of Severus, came to a sad end. Severus had such a strong character that though he tyrannized the people to keep the army friendly he was always able to govern with success; his qualities amazed and awed the people, impressed and pleased the army, so that both groups in their different ways admired him.

Since, for a man who took power rather than inheriting it, Severus achieved such a lot, I'd like very briefly to show how well he was able to play both the fox and the lion, animals that, as I said, a ruler must learn to imitate.

Aware that the emperor Julian was weak and indecisive, Severus persuaded the army he commanded in Slavonia to march on Rome and avenge Pertinax, who had been murdered by the Praetorian Guard. With this pretext and betraying no sign of any ambition to become emperor, he led his army towards Rome and was already in Italy before people realized he'd set out. When he arrived in Rome, the Senate, out of fear, elected him emperor and had Julian killed. Having got thus far, Severus faced two obstacles if he was to take complete control of the empire: one in Asia, where the commander of the Asian armies, Pescennius Niger, had declared himself emperor; and the other in the west, where Albinus also aspired to become emperor. Deciding it would be dangerous to show he was hostile to both opponents at once, Severus chose to attack Niger and trick Albinus. So he wrote to Albinus, in France, saying that now that the Senate had elected him emperor he wanted to share the honour with him, Albinus. He sent him the title of Caesar and had the Senate vote to make him co-emperor. Albinus was taken in, but as soon as Severus had defeated and killed Niger and got control of the eastern empire, he went back to Rome and complained in the Senate that Albinus, far from being grateful for everything Severus had given him, had set a trap to kill him; as a result, he, Severus, would have to go and punish his ingratitude. In fact he went to France, stripped Albinus of his power and had him killed.

If we look carefully at what Severus did, we find he played both the ferocious lion and the cunning fox very well; he was feared and respected by all parties and he managed to avoid being hated by the army. It's hardly surprising, then, that despite being a new arrival he was able to hold so much power: his enormous reputation always protected him from the hatred people might otherwise have felt as a result of his pillage and violence.

Severus's son, Antoninus, was also a man with some excellent qualities; the people thought him remarkable and the army welcomed him. He was a warlike leader, capable of handling every hardship and contemptuous of fine foods and easy living of any kind. So the army loved him. But his cruelty and ferocity were overwhelming and unspeakable, to the extent that, after endless individual murders, he wiped out much of the population of Rome and all the people of Alexandria. At this point everybody really hated him and even those close to him began to get nervous so that in the end he was killed by a centurion while among his soldiers.

It's worth noting that assassinations like this, coming as they do when a determined man takes a considered decision, are bound to happen to rulers sometimes, if only because, once a person no longer cares about dying, he's free to strike. That said, a ruler shouldn't be too concerned, because such murders are extremely rare. He must just take care not to do a serious injustice to any of the men he has serving him or keeps beside him to run the state. Antoninus in fact had killed the centurion's brother in disgraceful circumstances and was threatening the man himself every day, yet still kept him in his bodyguard. It was the kind of rash behaviour that can, and in this case did, lead to disaster.

But let's turn to Commodus, who could so easily have held on to the empire. Son of Marcus Aurelius, Commodus came to power by hereditary right; all he had to do was follow in his father's footsteps and he would have been welcome to army and people alike. But the man was cruel, bestially so, and to unleash his appetite and greed on the people he set about currying favour with the soldiers and corrupting them. He had no self-respect either and would often go down to the floor of the amphitheatre to fight the gladiators. He did so many things that were sordid and unworthy of an emperor that his soldiers found him contemptible, until, hated by the people and despised by the army, he eventually fell victim to a conspiracy.

Which leaves Maximinus. He was a real warmonger. As I said earlier on, the armies had been frustrated with the effeminate Alexander, and when they'd got rid of him they elected

Maximinus in his place. But he didn't last long. Two things led to his being both hated and despised. First, his extremely lowly background: he had been a shepherd in Thrace – everybody knew it and thought it scandalous; second, on becoming emperor he had put off going to Rome for the formal investiture and got himself a reputation for extreme cruelty by ordering his prefects in Rome and all over the empire to carry out numerous atrocities. Universally despised for his low birth, hated and feared for his ferocity, he faced rebellions first in Africa, then in the Senate; the Senate rebellion was supported by the entire population of Rome. Then the whole of Italy conspired against him, until finally his own army got involved; they were laying siege to Aquileia and finding it tough going; they were also fed up with his cruelty and when they realized how many enemies he had they became less afraid of the man and killed him.

I don't want to talk about Heliogabalus, Macrinus or Julian, who were all intensely despised and swiftly dispatched. Instead I'll conclude this discussion with the reflection that contemporary rulers do not have to give the same priority to satisfying the army that the Roman emperors did. True, one does have to pay the army some attention, but the problem is soon resolved, because none of today's rulers has to live with armies that have long experience in the government and administration of the provinces, as the armies of the Roman empire did. If the emperors had to put their armies before the people it was because the armies were the more powerful. These days it is more important for all rulers, with the exceptions of the Turkish and Egyptian sultans, to put the people before the army, because the people are more powerful.

I've made an exception of the Turkish leader because he keeps an army of 12,000 infantry and 15,000 cavalry beside him. Depending on them as he does for the strength and security of his realm he has to put their good will before any other consideration. In the same way, Egypt is entirely at the mercy of its army and again the sultan has to satisfy the soldiers before worrying about the people. It's worth noting that Egypt is a unique case; it is similar to the papal state, which can't be classified as a hereditary monarchy or as a new monarchy. When the old ruler dies he is not replaced by one of his children, but a new leader is elected by a body vested with this authority. Since the state's institutions are well established, this can hardly be compared with a situation where a new ruler seizes a state, and in fact a pope or Egyptian sultan faces none of the difficulties that a new ruler usually faces, because although he may be new to power the institutions are old and set up to work on his behalf as if he were a hereditary king.

But let's get back to our discussion. I'm sure that anyone reflecting on what I've said will see that it was hatred or contempt that led to the downfall of these Roman emperors; they will also understand how it was that, while some behaved one way and some another, there were nevertheless successes and failures in both groups. Since they had seized rather than inherited power, it was futile and dangerous for Pertinax and Alexander to try to imitate Marcus Aurelius, who had inherited his position; similarly, since they didn't have the necessary qualities, it was a fatal mistake for Caracalla, Commodus and Maximinus to imitate Severus. Though a man who has seized power and is establishing a new monarchy cannot imitate the likes of Marcus Aurelius, that doesn't mean he has to behave like Severus. What he must take from Severus are the policies you need to found a state, and from Marcus the policies that bring stability and glory once the state is firmly established.

20

Whether fortresses and other strategies rulers frequently adopt are useful

To hold power more securely, some rulers have disarmed their citizens; some have kept subject towns divided in factions; some have encouraged hostility towards themselves; others have sought to win over those who were initially suspicious of their rise to power; some have built fortresses; others have torn them down and destroyed them. And though one can't pass final judgement on these policies without detailed knowledge of the states where such decisions were taken, all the same I shall try to discuss the matter in general terms as far as is possible.

No one new to power has ever disarmed his subjects; on the contrary, finding them disarmed new rulers have always armed them. When you're the one giving people arms, those arms become yours; men who were potentially hostile become loyal, while those already loyal become your supporters rather than just your subjects. It's true you can't arm everyone, but in favouring some you can feel safer about the others too. Seeing that they've been preferred, the men you've armed will be under an obligation to you. The others won't be resentful, understanding that the people facing danger for you and binding their lives to yours will inevitably deserve the greater rewards. But when you take arms away from people, then you start to upset them; you show you don't trust them because you're frightened or cagey. Either way, they'll begin to hate you. Then, since you can hardly manage without an army, you'll have to turn to mercenary forces, which will have all the failings I discussed earlier. And even if your mercenaries are good, they'll never be good enough to defend you against powerful enemies and a hostile people.

So, as I said, a new ruler in a newly constituted state has always armed his subjects. History offers endless examples. But when a ruler acquires a new territory to add like an extra limb to an existing state, then he must disarm its people, except for the men who supported him when he took it. But with time and opportunity even those men should be kept weak and emasculated so that all the real armed force in the state as a whole resides with your own soldiers who live with you in your home base.

Generations ago, the experts in Florence used to say that you had to hold Pistoia by playing on its factions and Pisa by holding its fortresses. So they encouraged factionalism in some of the towns they held, the better to control them. In times when there was a certain balance between opposing parties in Italy this was probably an effective policy, but I don't think we should take it as a rule today. I don't think factional divisions ever really improved the situation. On the contrary, when an enemy approaches, a subject town that's divided in factions will fall at once. The weaker of the factions will always join forces with the attacker and the other faction won't be strong enough to beat them both.

The Venetians were reasoning along the same lines, I believe, when they fomented divisions between Guelphs and Ghibellines in the towns they held; they didn't let the factions get as far as bloodshed but encouraged divergences so that people would be too busy with their own disputes to unite against Venice. It wasn't, as things turned out, a successful policy. After the Venetians' defeat at Vailà, one or other of the factions immediately took courage and seized control of the various towns. This kind of policy actually indicates weakness on a ruler's part; in a healthy, confident state such differences would never be allowed; they are only useful in peacetime when they make it easier to keep people under control. In times of war everyone can see how flawed the policy is.

There's no doubt that rulers achieve greatness by overcoming the obstacles and enemies they find in their path. So when destiny wants to make a ruler great, particularly a new ruler who, unlike a hereditary king, really needs to build up his reputation, it sends him enemies and prompts them to attack him. That way he has the chance to beat them and climb the ladder his enemies have put in front of him. Hence many people reckon that when the opportunity presents itself a smart ruler will shrewdly provoke hostility so that he can then increase his reputation by crushing it.

Rulers, and especially those new to power, have found that men they initially doubted prove more loyal and useful than those they trusted. Pandolfo Petrucci ran Siena more with the men he had doubted than the others. But it's hard to lay down firm rules here because things vary from case to case. I'll just say this: that a ruler can very easily win over men who opposed him when he came to power, if they are not in a position to support themselves with their own resources. They'll be forced to behave more loyally than others in that they know they have to work hard to offset the negative impression the ruler initially had of them. So a ruler can always get more out of such men than out of people who feel too safe in his service and don't really make an effort.

Since the discussion demands it, I wouldn't like to leave out a reminder to any ruler who has taken a new state with inside help that he must think hard about why the local people who helped him did so. If they didn't act out of natural friendship for the new ruler, but only because the previous government wasn't giving them what they wanted, it will be extremely demanding and difficult to keep their support, because the new ruler won't be able to give them what they want either. Looking carefully at the reasons for this and drawing on the examples available from ancient and modern history, we find that it is much easier to win over those who were content with the previous government, and hence your enemies, than the men who were not content and so made an alliance with you and helped you take the country.

One way rulers have tried to secure their power is by building fortresses to curb and discourage potential aggressors and to offer a safe refuge in case of sudden attack. I approve of this policy, if only because it has been used for centuries. All the same, there is the recent example of Niccolò Vitelli who demolished two fortresses in Città di Castello in order to hold the town. When Guidobaldo retook possession of his lands after Cesare Borgia's occupation, he razed every fortress in the state to the ground, convinced that he'd be less likely to lose it again without them. And when the Bentivoglio family returned to power in Bologna it did the same thing. So, whether fortresses are useful or not will depend on the circumstances; in one situation they'll be a help and in another they'll be dangerous. We can sum up the reasons for this as follows.

The ruler who is more afraid of his people than of foreign enemies must build fortresses; but the ruler who is more afraid of foreign enemies should do without them. The castle Francesco Sforza built in Milan has provoked and will go on provoking more rebellions against the Sforza family than any other cause of unrest in the whole state. Your best fortress is not to be hated by the people, because even if you do have fortresses, they won't save you if the people hate you. Once the people have decided to take up arms against you they'll never be short of foreign support. In recent times there are no examples of fortresses having proved useful to any ruler at all, with the exception of the Countess of Forlì, Caterina Sforza, when her husband, Count Girolamo Riario, was murdered. Taking refuge in the fortress, she was able to survive the rebels' assault, wait till help came from Milan, then take control again. Circumstances were such at the time that no foreign enemies were in a position to help the people. Later, however, her fortresses were not much use when Cesare Borgia attacked the town, and the people, who were hostile to her, fought on his side. Both then and earlier she would have been safer had she avoided making an enemy of the people rather than counting on fortresses. All things considered, I'll give my approval both to rulers who build fortresses and to those who don't, but I'll always criticize any ruler who imagines it doesn't matter whether the people hate him or not and trusts in fortresses for his security.

21

What a ruler should do to win respect

Nothing wins a ruler respect like great military victories and a display of remarkable personal qualities. One example in our own times is Ferdinand of Aragon, the present King of Spain. One might almost describe him as a ruler new to power because from being a weak king he has become the most famous and honoured of Christendom, and when you look at his achievements you find they are all remarkable and some of them extraordinary. At the beginning of his reign he launched an invasion of Granada, a campaign that laid the foundation of his power. It was important that he did it at a moment of domestic quiet when he didn't have to worry about possible interruptions: the war then kept the Castilian barons busy so that they didn't start plotting changes inside Spain. Meanwhile, and without their even noticing, Ferdinand's power and reputation were increasing at their expense. Supplying his armies with money from the Church and the people, he was able to sustain a long war that allowed him to establish, then consolidate, a military force that would do him proud in the future. After that was done, to ensure the Church's support for even larger campaigns, he perpetrated an act of cruelty dressed up as piety, stripping the Marrano Jews of their wealth and expelling them from his kingdom, a move that could hardly have been more distressing or striking. Once again under cover of religion, he attacked Africa, then moved into Italy and finally attacked France. So he was always planning and doing great things, keeping his people in a state of suspense and admiration, concentrated as they were on the outcome of his various campaigns. Since each of these came as a consequence of the one before, he never gave the more powerful men in the country any slack time between wars when they could plot against him.

A leader can also win acclaim by giving impressive demonstrations of character in his handling of domestic affairs, as Bernabò Visconti did in Milan; whenever anyone does anything remarkable, whether for good or ill, in civil life, you think up some reward or punishment that will cause a stir. But above all a ruler must make sure that everything he does gives people the impression that he is a great man of remarkable abilities.

A ruler will also be respected when he is a genuine friend and a genuine enemy, that is, when he declares himself unambiguously for one side and against the other. This policy will always bring better results than neutrality. For example, if you have two powerful neighbours who go to war, you may or may not have reason to fear the winner afterwards. Either way it will always be better to take sides and fight hard. If you do have cause to fear but stay neutral, you'll still be gobbled up by the winner to the amusement and satisfaction of the loser; you'll have no excuses, no defence and nowhere to hide. Because a winner doesn't want half-hearted friends who don't help him in a crisis; and the loser will have nothing to do with you since you didn't choose to fight alongside him and share his fate.

When Antiochus was sent to Greece by the Aetolians to push back the Romans, he sent ambassadors to the Achaeans, who were allied to the Romans, asking them to remain neutral, while for their part the Romans encouraged them to join the war on their side. The Achaean council debated the matter and after Antiochus's ambassador had spoken, asking them to remain neutral, the Roman ambassador replied: 'With regard to this invitation to remain neutral, nothing could be more damaging to your interests: you'll get no thanks, no consideration and will be taken as a reward by whoever wins.'

The contender who is not your ally will always try to get you to stay neutral and your ally will always try to get you to fight. Indecisive rulers who want to avoid immediate danger usually decide to stay neutral, and usually things end badly for them. But if you declare yourself courageously for one side or the other and your ally wins, he'll be indebted to you and there'll be a bond of friendship between you, so that even if he is more powerful now and has you at his mercy he's not going to be so shameless as to take advantage of the circumstances and become an example of ingratitude. Victories are never so decisive that the winner can override every principle, justice in particular. But if your ally loses, you're still his friend and he'll offer what help he can: you become companions in misfortune, and your luck could always turn.

In the event that the two neighbours going to war are not so powerful that you need fear the winner, it is even more sensible to take sides and get involved: you'll be destroying one with the help of another who, if he had any sense, would be protecting the loser. And when your ally wins, which with your help is inevitable, he'll be at your mercy.

Here it's worth noting that a ruler must never ally himself with someone more powerful in order to attack his enemies, unless, as I said above, it is absolutely necessary. Because when you win you'll be at your ally's mercy, and whenever possible rulers must avoid placing themselves in another's power. The Venetians allied themselves with France to attack the Duke of Milan. It was an alliance they could have avoided and it led to disaster. But when such an alliance can't be avoided, as was the case with Florence when the pope and Spain took their armies to attack Lombardy, then a ruler must take sides for the reasons set out above. In general, a ruler must never imagine that any decision he takes is safe; on the contrary he should reckon that any decision is potentially dangerous. It is in the nature of things that every time you try to avoid one danger you run into another. Good sense consists in being able to assess the dangers and choose the lesser of various evils.

A ruler must also show that he admires achievement in others, giving work to men of ability and rewarding people who excel in this or that craft. What's more, he should reassure his subjects that they can go calmly about their business as merchants or farmers, or whatever other trade they practise, without worrying that if they increase their wealth they'll be in danger of having it taken away from them, or that if they start up a business they'll be punitively taxed. On the contrary, a ruler should offer incentives to people who want to do this kind of thing and to whoever plans to bring prosperity to his city or state. Then at the right times of the year he should entertain people with shows and festivals. And since every city is divided into guilds and districts, he should respect these groups and go to their meetings from time to time, showing what a humane and generous person he is, though without ever forgetting the authority of his position, something he must always keep to the fore.

22

A ruler's ministers

A ruler's choice of ministers is an important matter. The quality of the ministers will reflect his good sense or lack of it and give people their first impression of the way the ruler's mind is working. If his ministers are capable and loyal, people will always reckon a ruler astute, because he was able to recognize their ability and command their loyalty. When they are not, people will always have reason to criticize, because the first mistake the ruler made was in his choice of ministers. Everyone who knew Antonio da Venafro, Pandolfo Petrucci's minister in Siena, thought Pandolfo extremely smart for having chosen him.

There are actually three kinds of mind: one kind grasps things unaided, the second sees what another has grasped, the third grasps nothing and sees nothing. The first kind is extremely valuable, the second valuable, the third useless. So although Pandolfo didn't have the first kind of mind, he certainly had the second; if someone is sharp enough to recognize what's right and wrong in what another man says and does, then even if he doesn't have the creativity to make policy himself, he can still see which of his minister's policies are positive and negative, encourage the good ones and correct the bad. The minister, meanwhile, will realize that he can't fool the ruler and so will have to behave.

There is one infallible way of checking a minister's credentials: when you see the man thinking more for himself than for you, when his policies are all designed to enhance his own interests, then he'll never make a good minister and you'll never be able to trust him. A minister running a state must never think of himself, only of the ruler, and should concentrate exclusively on the ruler's business. To make sure he does so, the ruler, for his part, must take an interest in the minister, grant him wealth and respect, oblige him and share honours and appointments with him. That way the minister will see that he can't survive without the ruler. He'll have so many honours he won't want any more, so much wealth he won't look for more, and so many appointments that he'll guard against any change of the status quo. When rulers and their ministers arrange their relationships this way, they can trust each other. When they don't, one or the other is bound to come to a bad end.

23

Avoiding flatterers

There's another important issue we need to consider, a mistake rulers can only avoid if they are very canny, or very good at choosing their ministers. I'm talking about flatterers. Courts are always full of them and men are so ready to congratulate themselves on their achievements and to imagine themselves more successful than they are that it is hard not to fall into this error. Then if you do try to defend yourself from flatterers you run the risk of having people despise you. Because the only way to guard against flattery is to have people understand that you don't mind them telling you the truth. But when anyone and everyone can tell you the truth, you lose respect.

So the sensible ruler must find a middle way, choosing intelligent men for ministers and giving them and only them the right to tell him the truth, and only on the issues he asks about, not in general. However, the ruler should ask his ministers about everything and listen to their opinions, then make up his mind on his own, following his own criteria. In responding to these advisers, as a group or separately, he should make it clear that the more openly they speak, the more welcome their advice will be. After which, he shouldn't take advice from anyone else, but get on with whatever has been decided and be firm in his decisions. Try a different approach and you'll either be ruined by flatterers or change your mind so often listening to everyone's opinions that people will lose their respect for you.

Let me offer an example from modern times. Bishop Luca Rainaldi, a man close to the present Emperor Maximilian, said that the emperor never took advice from anyone and never got his own policies enacted; this is because he did the opposite of what I proposed above. Being secretive, the emperor tends not to explain his plans to anyone and doesn't seek advice. But when he starts putting his policies into action and people see what he's up to, his ministers tell him he's got it wrong and all too readily he changes his mind. As a result, whatever he does one day he undoes the next and nobody understands what he wants or means to do and no one can make plans in response to his policies.

So a ruler must always take advice, but only when he wants it, not when others want to give it to him. In fact he should discourage people from giving him advice unasked. On the other hand he should ask a great deal and listen patiently when an adviser responds truthfully. And if he realizes someone is keeping quiet out of fear, he should show his irritation. Many people think that when a ruler has a reputation for being sensible it's thanks to the good advice he's getting from his ministers and not because he's shrewd himself. But they're wrong. There's a general and infallible rule here: that a leader who isn't sensible himself can never get good advice, unless he just happens to have put the government entirely in the hands of a single minister who turns out to be extremely shrewd. In this case he may well get good advice, but the situation won't last long because the minister will soon grab the state for himself. If on the other hand he's taking advice from more than one person, an ingenuous ruler will find himself listening to very different opinions and won't know how to make sense of them. Each of his advisers will be thinking of his own interests and the ruler won't be able to control them or even sense what's going on. It's not a case of finding better ministers; men will always be out to trick you unless you force them to be honest. In conclusion: a ruler isn't smart because he's getting proper advice; on the contrary, it's his good sense that makes the right advice possible.

24

Why Italian rulers have lost their states

Followed carefully, the guidelines I've laid down will allow a ruler who's just taken over a state to assume the aura of a hereditary king and give him even greater security and staying power than if his government was well established. People watch what a new ruler does far more attentively than they do a hereditary one and if his achievements are impressive they'll have a greater hold on people and command greater loyalty than an old royal bloodline. Men are more interested in the present than the past and when things are going well they'll be happy and won't look elsewhere; on the contrary, they'll do everything they can to defend a ruler so long as he doesn't let himself down in other ways. So he'll enjoy the double glory of having both founded a new kingdom and graced and consolidated it with good laws, a good army, good allies and good policies. Conversely, the man who's born to power but behaves so stupidly as to lose it is shamed twice over.

Turning now to those Italian rulers who've lost power in recent years – the King of Naples, for example, and the Duke of Milan and others too – the first thing we find is that they all had poor armies, this for the reasons I discussed at length above. Then we see that some of them had the people against them, or if they did have the people's support they couldn't keep the nobles on their side. Without these failings you don't lose a state that's strong enough to field an army. Philip of

Macedonia – not Alexander's father but the Philip beaten by Titus Quintius – had nothing like the resources of the Romans and Greeks who attacked him: all the same, being a military man and a leader who knew how to please the people and keep the nobles on his side, he held out for many years and though in the end he did lose control of a few towns, at least he hung on to his kingdom.

So these rulers of ours, who were well-established kings and dukes yet still lost their states, should spare us their bad-luck stories; they have only themselves to blame. In peacetime they never imagined anything could change (it's a common shortcoming not to prepare for the storm while the weather is fair) and when trouble struck their first thought was to run for it rather than defend themselves; they hoped the people would be incensed by the barbarity of the invaders and call them back. This isn't a bad policy when you have no alternative, but to trust in that reaction when you could have taken other precautions is a serious failing; a ruler should never be resigned to falling from power because he's counting on finding someone to prop him up again afterwards. Maybe people won't oblige, and even if they do, you won't be safe, because your strategy was spineless and involved relying on others. The only good, sure, lasting forms of defence are those based on yourself and your own strength.

25

The role of luck in human affairs, and how to defend against it

I realize that many people have believed and still do believe that the world is run by God and by fortune and that however shrewd men may be they can't do anything about it and have no way of protecting themselves. As a result they may decide that it's hardly worth making an effort and just leave events to chance. This attitude is more prevalent these days as a result of the huge changes we've witnessed and are still witnessing every day, things that no one could have predicted. Sometimes, thinking it over, I have leaned a bit that way myself.

All the same, and so as not to give up on our free will, I reckon it may be true that luck decides the half of what we do, but it leaves the other half, more or less, to us. It's like one of those raging rivers that sometimes rise and flood the plain, tearing down trees and buildings, dragging soil from one place and dumping it down in another. Everybody runs for safety, no one can resist the rush, there's no way you can stop it. Still, the fact that a river is like this doesn't prevent us from preparing for trouble when levels are low, building banks and dykes, so that when the water rises the next time it can be contained in a single channel and the rush of the river in flood is not so uncontrolled and destructive.

Fortune's the same. It shows its power where no one has taken steps to contain it, flooding into places where it finds neither banks nor dykes that can hold it back. And if you look at Italy, which has been both the scene of revolutionary changes and the agent that set them in motion, you'll see it's a land that has neither banks nor dykes to protect it. Had the country been properly protected, like Germany, Spain and France, either the flood wouldn't have had such drastic effects or it wouldn't have happened at all.

I think that is all that need be said in general terms about how to deal with the problem of luck.

Going into detail, though, we've all seen how a ruler may be doing well one day and then lose power the next without any apparent change in his character or qualities. I believe this is mostly due to the attitude I mentioned above: that is, the ruler trusts entirely to luck and collapses when it changes. I'm also convinced that the successful ruler is the one who adapts to changing times; while the leader who fails does so because his approach is out of step with circumstances.

All men want glory and wealth, but they set out to achieve those goals in different ways. Some are cautious, others impulsive; some use violence, others finesse; some are patient, others quite the opposite. And all these different approaches can be successful. It's also true that two men can both be cautious but with different results: one is successful and the other fails. Or again you see two men being equally successful but with different approaches, one cautious, the other impulsive. This depends entirely on whether their approach suits the circumstances, which in turn is why, as I said, two men with different approaches may both succeed while, of two with the same approach, one may succeed and the other not.

This explains why people's fortunes go up and down. If someone is behaving cautiously and patiently and the times and circumstances are such that the approach works, he'll be successful. But if times and circumstances change, everything goes wrong for him, because he hasn't changed his approach to match. You won't find anyone shrewd enough to adapt his character like this, in part because you can't alter your natural bias and in part because, if a person has always been successful with a particular approach, he won't easily be persuaded to drop it. So when the time comes for the cautious man to act impulsively, he can't, and he comes unstuck. If he did change personality in line with times and circumstances, his luck would hold steady.

Pope Julius II always acted impulsively and lived in times and circumstances so well suited to this approach that things always went well for him. Think of his first achievement, taking Bologna while Giovanni Bentivoglio was still alive. The Venetians were against the idea, the King of Spain likewise, and Julius was still negotiating the matter with the French. All the same, and with his usual ferocity and impetuousness, the pope set out and led the expedition himself. This put the Venetians and Spanish in a quandary and they were unable to react, the Venetians out of fear and the Spanish because they hoped to recover the whole of the Kingdom of Naples. Meanwhile, the King of France was brought on board: he needed Rome as an ally to check the Venetians and decided that once Julius had made his move he couldn't deny him armed support without too obviously slighting him.

With this impulsive decision, then, Julius achieved more than any other pope with all the good sense in the world would ever have achieved. Had he waited to have everything arranged and negotiated before leaving Rome, as any other pope would have done, the plan would never have worked. The King of France would have come up with endless excuses and the Venetians and Spanish with endless warnings. I don't want to go into Julius's other campaigns, which were all of a kind and all successful. His early death spared him the experience of failure. Because if times had changed and circumstances demanded caution, he would have been finished. The man would never have changed his ways, because they were natural to him.

To conclude then: fortune varies but men go on regardless.

When their approach suits the times they're successful, and when it doesn't they're not. My opinion on the matter is this: it's better to be impulsive than cautious; fortune is female and if you want to stay on top of her you have to slap and thrust. You'll see she's more likely to yield that way than to men who go about her coldly. And being a woman she likes her men young, because they're not so cagey, they're wilder and more daring when they master her.

26

An appeal to conquer Italy and free it from foreign occupation

Going back over everything I've said, I've been asking myself whether the time is right, in Italy now, for a new ruler; whether there's the sort of material available here that would give a shrewd man with the right qualities the chance to impose some form, winning honour for himself and doing good to the people as a whole. And my impression is that a lot of things are running the way of a new man, so many in fact that I don't know what time was ever more right than the present. If, as I said earlier, Moses could only emerge after the people of Israel had been enslaved in Egypt, Cyrus show his great spirit after the Persians were crushed by the Medes, Theseus prove his excellence after the Athenians were defeated and dispersed, so today, for us to witness the qualities of a great Italian, the country had to be reduced to its present state: more slave than the Jews, more crushed than the Persians, more divided than the Athenians, leaderless, lawless, beaten, plundered, broken and overrun, ruined in every way.

There was one man* who showed glimpses of greatness, the kind of thing that made you think he was sent by God for the country's redemption, but then at the height of his achievements his luck turned. So now Italy lies, half-dead, waiting to see who will heal her wounds and put an end to the devastation of Lombardy, the extortionate taxation of

* Presumably Borgia.

Tuscany and Naples, who will clean up the sores that have festered too long. You can see the country is praying God to send someone to save her from the cruelty and barbarity of these foreigners. You can see she is ready and willing to march beneath a flag, if only someone would raise one up.

What I can't see is any family the country could put its faith in right now if not your illustrious house,* blessed as it is with fine qualities and fortune, favoured by God and the Church – actually running the Church, in fact – and hence well placed to lead Italy to redemption. And if you keep in mind the lives and achievements of the men I've written about, then the project won't be too difficult. It's true they were rare men, remarkable men, but nevertheless they were still men, and none of them had a better opportunity than you have now. The things they did had no greater justification, nor were they any easier; God was no kinder to them than he has been to you. Justice is definitely on our side because 'war is just when there's no alternative and arms are sacred when they are your only hope.' The situation is more than favourable, and when circumstances are favourable things can't be too hard; all you have to do is take the men I've proposed as your models. What's more, God has shown us amazing, unprecedented signs: the sea parted; a cloud led the way for you; stone has gushed water; manna has rained on us from heaven; everything has worked together to make you great. The rest is up to you. God doesn't like doing everything himself, he doesn't want to deprive us of our free will and our share of glory.

It's no surprise if none of the Italians I've spoken about have been able to do what I believe your family can do, or again if all our recent wars and revolutions have given the impression that the country has lost its capacity to fight. This is because the old states were badly organized and no one knew how to improve things. Nothing brings more honour

* Machiavelli is addressing Lorenzo de' Medici.

to a new ruler than the new laws and institutions he intro-
duces. When they are well thought out and show vision they
bring a ruler respect and admiration. Italy is hardly lacking
in raw material for the man who wants to give form to it. The
limbs are healthy and strong; all they need is a head to guide
them. Look how much stronger, defter and more skilful
Italians are than foreigners in duels or small skirmishes. But
when it comes to armies they can't compete. Because they are
badly led. The capable men are ignored, the incapable are
convinced they are capable, and to date no one has had the
talent and luck to score the sort of success that would force
the others to stand aside. That's why in all these wars over
the past twenty years, whenever an army has been entirely
made up of Italians it has always failed miserably, as witness
first the battle of Taro, then those of Alessandria, Capua,
Genova, Vailà, Bologna and Mestre.

So if your illustrious family should choose to follow in the
steps of those excellent men who came to the rescue of their
peoples, the first thing that needs to be done, the real foundation of any such achievement, is to establish an army of
your own citizens. You can't have more loyal, determined
and better soldiers than your own. And if each man taken
singly is good, when they're all together and find themselves
led, fed and respected by their own ruler they'll be even better.
Founding an army like this is absolutely essential if we
are to use Italian mettle to defend ourselves against foreign
enemies.

It's true that the Swiss and Spanish infantries are thought
to be formidable, but both have weak points that would allow
a third force not only to face them but to feel confident of
beating them. The Spanish can't stand up to cavalry and the
Swiss are in trouble when they run into infantry as determined
as themselves. That's why, as we've seen and will see again,
the Spanish can't turn back a French cavalry attack and the
Swiss collapse in front of a Spanish-style infantry. And though

we haven't had complete proof of this Swiss vulnerability, we got a glimpse of it at the battle of Ravenna when the Spanish infantry took on the Germans, who use the same tactics as the Swiss. Relying on their agility and their small round shields, the Spanish got under the German pikes, where, safe themselves, they could strike at will. At this point the Germans were helpless and if the cavalry hadn't turned up to push the Spanish back they'd all have been killed. Knowing the weak points of these two armies, then, it's quite possible to train a new army that could hold back a cavalry attack and wouldn't be unsettled by infantry combat: it's a question of what weapons you have and what new tactics you can invent. These are the kinds of developments that enhance a new ruler's reputation and bring him great prestige.

It would be a big mistake, then, after all this time, to pass up the chance of rescuing Italy. Words can't express the loving welcome such a saviour would get in all the towns that have suffered from this torrent of foreign invaders: the thirst for revenge, the unswerving trust, the devotion, the tears. What doors would be closed to such a man? Who would refuse to obey him? What envy could stand in his way? What Italian would not bow his knee? Everybody loathes this barbarous occupation. So, may your noble house undertake this duty with the spirit and hope that inspire just causes, so that our country may be glorified under your banner, and under your protection Petrarch's words be fulfilled:

> Virtue against fury
> Shall take up arms; and the fight be short;
> For ancient valour
> Is not dead in Italian hearts.*

* Virtù contro a furore
  Prenderà l'arme; e fia el combatter corto;
  Ché l'antico valore
  Nelli italici cor non è ancor morto.

Glossary of Proper Names

Machiavelli would have expected his readers to be familiar with the exploits of the men he mentions from contemporary and modern times, while they would not have known so much about some of the figures he cites from ancient history. In an attempt to put today's reader in something of the same position, I have been more generous with information on the figures from modern history, and less so with those from Roman times and before.

ACHILLES   Greek hero in the Trojan War, son of the immortal nymph Thetis and raised by Chiron the centaur.

ACUTO, GIOVANNI   Italianization of John Hawkwood (1320–94). Having served in the English army in France, in 1360 Hawkwood joined mercenary soldiers in Burgundy and later commanded the so-called White Company fighting for different states and factions in Italy. Constantly playing off his employers against their enemies, he built up considerable wealth. From 1390 on he commanded Florentine armies in their war against the Viscontis of Milan.

AGATHOCLES (361–289 BC)   Ruler of Syracuse (317–289 BC) and King of Sicily (304–289 BC). Seized power in Syracuse, exiling and murdering thousands in the process. His formation of a strong army and domination of Sicily led to protracted conflict with Carthage.

ALBINUS   Decimus Clodius Ceionius Septimius (c.150–197). Roman military commander in Britain who proclaimed himself emperor on the murder of Pertinax in 193. Albinus initially allied himself with Severus in Rome who had also proclaimed himself emperor, but the two fell out and in 197, having lost the Battle of Lugdunum (modern Lyons), Albinus either killed himself or was killed.

ALEXANDER   Alexander the Great (356–323 BC), King of Macedonia (336–323 BC). He conquered Greece, Persia, and much of Asia.

ALEXANDER   Marcus Aurelius Alexander Severus (208–235), Roman emperor (222–235). Adopted as his heir in 221 by the emperor Heliogabalus, who was also his first cousin, Alexander was eventually murdered by his own soldiers.

ALEXANDER VI   Rodrigo Borgia (1431–1503). Born in Valencia with the Spanish surname Borja, later Italianized to Borgia. Elected pope in 1492, Alexander openly recognized as many as eight illegitimate children, all of whom he tried to place in high positions. The most famous were Cesare Borgia and Lucrezia Borgia. Involved in endless intrigues to extend his territories and increase his wealth, Alexander was considered the most corrupt and grasping of the Renaissance popes. Although frequently accused of murder, usually by poison, there is no evidence that his own sudden illness and death in 1503 were the result of poisoning.

ANTIOCHUS   Antiochus the Great (c.241–187 BC), King of Syria (223–187 BC). Spent most of his reign in military campaigns rebuilding the state he had inherited and conquering much of Asia Minor. In 192 BC he invaded Greece but was beaten by the Romans and eventually lost Asia Minor to them as well.

ANTONINUS CARACALLA   see CARACALLA.

ASCANIO   See SFORZA, CARDINAL.

BAGLIONI   The Baglioni family ruled Perugia, a town midway between Florence and Rome, in the fifteenth and sixteenth centuries.

BENTIVOGLI, GIOVANNI (1438–1508)   Son of Annibale, ruler of Bologna, who was murdered in 1445 when Giovanni was just a child. After a long interregnum Giovanni eventually took his father's place in 1462, but was forced to flee when Pope Julius II attacked the town in 1506.

BERGAMO, BARTOLOMEO DA   Bartolomeo Colleone (c.1395–1475). Mercenary leader in the service of Venice and commander of Venetian forces against Milan after Carmagnola was killed. Colleone was remarkable for not changing sides or seeking to play one side off against another. He is celebrated in the famous Colleone monument by Andrea Verocchio in Venice, which shows the leader on his horse.

BERNABÒ See VISCONTI.

BORGIA, CESARE (c.1475–1507) Illegitimate son of Cardinal Rodrigo Borgia, later Pope Alexander VI, Cesare Borgia was made Bishop of Pamplona at fifteen and a cardinal at eighteen. In 1497 the murder of his elder brother Giovanni made him the main beneficiary of his father's plans for territorial expansion. Cesare was suspected of Giovanni's murder but nothing was proved. In 1498 he negotiated with Louis XII in Paris on behalf of his father; the king's marriage was dissolved, allowing him to marry the widow of Charles VIII, while Louis agreed to an aggressive military alliance with the pope to capture Naples. Cesare then became the first person in history to resign his position as cardinal, upon which Louis made him Duke of Valentinois, hence the nickname, Duke Valentino. The alliance with Louis was reinforced by Borgia's marriage to Charlotte d'Albret, the king's cousin, and Borgia was serving with Louis's army when it captured Milan in 1499. Prompted by his father and with Louis's military support, Borgia set out to conquer the Romagna, taking the towns of Fano, Pesaro, Rimini, Cesena, Forlì, Faenza and Imola. In 1501 the pope declared him Duke of Romagna. Borgia successfully commanded French troops at the siege of Naples in 1501, returning to the Romagna to capture Urbino and Camerino in 1502. In this period he appointed Leonardo da Vinci as his military architect and engineer. Faced with a revolt by mercenary leaders in his service, he invited them to Senigallia to negotiate and had them imprisoned and executed. The death of his father in 1503 eventually led to the loss of the Romagna, imprisonment and exile to Spain, where Borgia died in the service of his brother-in-law King John III of Navarre.

BORGIA, RODRIGO See ALEXANDER VI.

BORGIA, VALENTINO Duke Valentino. See BORGIA, CESARE.

BRACCIO Andrea Braccio da Montone (1368–1424). Successful mercenary commander who fought numerous campaigns both for and against most of the major states in Italy, eventually becoming ruler of Perugia.

CAESAR   Julius Caesar (c.100–44 BC). After successful military campaigns in Gaul and Britain, Julius Caesar made himself dictator, taking the first step to transforming the Roman Republic into the Roman Empire. He was assassinated by a group of senators including his former friend Marcus Junius Brutus.

CANNESCHI   A family that vied with the Bentivogli family for power in Bologna. The Bentivoglis were supported by Venice and Florence while the Canneschis were allied to the Viscontis, dukes of Milan. In 1445, with Milanese support, Battista Canneschi, head of the family, had Annibale Bentivogli murdered. The people of Bologna, however, turned against the Canneschis and lynched Battista, after which the rest of the family fled.

CARACALLA   Marcus Aurelius Antoninus Caracalla (188–217), Roman emperor (211–217). On the death of his father, the emperor Severus, Antoninus took power with his brother Geta, but soon had him murdered, together with all his supporters. He extended Roman citizenship to all free citizens of the empire, keeping the support of the army by increasing soldiers' pay. Unpopular with the people, Antoninus was eventually murdered by a member of his own guard, perhaps on the instigation of Macrinus, the next emperor.

CARMAGNOLA   Francesco Bussone (c.1432–82), Count of Carmagnola, a small town near Turin. Carmagnola was a mercenary leader hired first by Duke Visconti of Milan, then later by the Venetians to fight Milan. Failing to follow up an initial victory at the battle of Maclodio in 1427, Carmagnola was accused of treachery, arrested and beheaded.

CHARLES VII (1403–61)   King of France (1422–61). Inspired by Joan of Arc, Charles united France under one ruler, driving the English from all their French possessions with the exception of Calais. He built up a powerful standing army.

CHARLES VIII (1470–98)   King of France (1483–98). Having taken effective power in 1492 after the regency of his sister Anne and encouraged by both the pope and Ludovico Sforza, Duke of Milan, to assert his claim to the throne of Naples, Charles assembled an army of 25,000 men and in 1494 marched into

Italy. Having subdued Naples' ally, Florence, Charles took Naples itself in 1495. At this point the other Italian powers, including the pope and Duke Ludovico, turned against him and drove him out of the peninsula.

COLONNA, CARDINAL   Giovanni Colonna. Made a cardinal in 1480, Giovanni plotted with Charles VIII against Alexander VI.

COLONNA   A powerful family in medieval and Renaissance Rome, notorious for their long feud with the Orsini family. The Colonna family produced one pope, Martin V (ruled 1417–31), but were later excommunicated and their estates confiscated by Alexander VI. The feud between the families was ended by papal bull in 1511.

COMMODUS   Lucius Aurelius Commodus Antoninus (161–193), Roman emperor (180–93). The son of Marcus Aurelius, Commodus rejected his father's stoic asceticism, giving himself over to pleasure and amusement while allowing a series of favourites to run the empire. Boastful about his physique, he regularly took part in naked gladiatorial combat. Eventually a conspiracy against him led to his being strangled by the wrestler Narcissus.

CONIO, ALBERIGO DA   Alberigo da Barbiano (c.1348–1409) was originally from the Romagna but later became Count of Conio, a small town in the hills above the Italian Riviera. He was the first mercenary commander to insist that his army (the Company of St George) be made up exclusively of Italians, a development that led to a reduction in the use of foreign mercenaries. Alberigo fought for Milan against Florence, dying in battle in 1409.

CYRUS (c.576–529 BC)   Founder of the Persian empire, which he extended to include much of central and south-west Asia.

DARIUS   Last king of Persia (336–331 BC), Darius was repeatedly defeated in battle by Alexander the Great and finally deposed and murdered by one of his provincial governors.

DAVID (c.1012–972 BC)   The second King of Israel (after Saul, his father). Famous for his legendary defeat of the Philistine giant Goliath, using only a sling and stones. As king, David built up an empire, capturing Jerusalem, which he made his capital, as well as areas of modern Jordan and Syria.

EPAMINONDAS (418–362 BC)   Theban statesman and military

commander, he ended Spartan pre-eminence in Greece, making Thebes the dominant power.

FABIUS MAXIMUS (*c*.280–203 BC)   Statesman and military commander, five times consul and twice dictator of Rome. Famous for his cautious delaying tactics against Hannibal in the Second Punic War and his hostility towards Scipio.

FERDINAND OF ARAGON (1452–1516)   At age seventeen Ferdinand married Isabella of Castile, then eighteen, thus taking a first step towards uniting Spain. He ruled Castile with his wife from 1474 and became King of Aragon in 1479. After a long campaign to capture Granada, the last territory held by the Muslims in Spain, Ferdinand was finally victorious in 1492. In the same year he expelled the Jews from both Castile and Aragon. The second half of his reign was spent countering French expansionism in Italy. From 1494 to 1496 he aided Italian leaders in their battle to drive Charles VIII of France out of Italy. In 1501 he signed an agreement with Louis XII to split the Kingdom of Naples between them, but later turned against France, capturing the whole of the kingdom by 1504. By the time of his death, Spain was the most powerful country in Europe, a power enhanced when Ferdinand was succeeded by his grandson, Charles of Austria, who was also Holy Roman Emperor.

FERRARA, DUKE OF   Machiavelli is actually referring to two dukes in a family that had ruled Ferrara for some four centuries. (1) Ercole d'Este (1431–1505), duke from 1471–1505. Educated in Naples, Ercole married the daughter of King Ferrante of Naples and became one of the great patrons of Renaissance art. In 1481, in alliance with Ferrante, he fought against the Venetians and the papacy, losing a considerable amount of territory. He remained neutral in the so-called Italian War of 1494–98, but after the French took Milan in 1499 he asked for and was granted French protection.

(2) Alfonso d'Este (1476–34), duke from 1505–34. Alfonso married, first, Anna Sforza, sister of Gian Galeazzo Sforza and, later, Lucrezia Borgia, daughter of Pope Alexander VI. In 1508 he joined the League of Cambrai, which sought to destroy Venetian power and partition its territories. After Pope Julius II went over to the Venetian side, Alfonso remained loyal to France, as a result

of which he was excommunicated and attacked by both Venice
and the papacy. He resisted successfully, partly thanks to French
help, and partly due to Ferrara's superior cannons whose manu-
facture was a matter of special concern and pride to the duke. In
1526–27 Alfonso took part in the expedition of Charles V (Holy
Roman Emperor and King of Spain) which led to the sacking of
Rome.

FILIPPO, DUKE   See VISCONTI, FILIPPO.

FOGLIANI, GIOVANNI   A leading citizen of Fermo, Fogliani was
killed in 1501.

FORLÌ, COUNTESS OF   Caterina Sforza (1463–1509), an illegitimate daughter of Galeazzo Sforza, Duke of Milan. She married
Girolamo Riario, officially the nephew but possibly the son of
Pope Sixtus IV. Riario was Count of Forlì and after his murder
in 1488 Caterina took control of the town until it was captured
by Cesare Borgia in 1500. She is famous for having refused to
hand over the citadel of Forlì to rebels despite their threatening
to kill her children, whom they held hostage. Exposing her gen-
itals from the castle walls, she told them she was perfectly capable
of producing more children.

GRACCHI, THE   The brothers Tiberius Gracchus and Gaius Sem-
pronius Gracchus were members of a prominent family in Rome
in the second century BC. Both became Tribunes of the Plebs and
both were murdered after attempting to limit the power of the
nobles and introduce reforms in favour of the plebs.

GUIDOBALDO, DUKE OF URBINO (1472–1508)   Guidobaldo
da Montefeltro succeeded his father as Duke of Urbino in 1482.
He fought as a military captain for Pope Alexander VI and
Charles VIII of France, and later for Venice against Charles.
Under attack from Cesare Borgia in 1497, he fled the town,
returning when Borgia's mercenaries proved disloyal. Under
Guidobaldo's rule, the court of Urbino was among the most
refined in Europe and is considered to have been the inspiration
of Baldassare Castiglione's *Book of the Courtier*, which discusses
the qualities of the perfect courtier.

HAMILCAR   Hamilcar Barca (c.270–228 BC). Successful commander of the Carthaginians in the First Punic War against
Roman forces in Sicily in 247 BC. Launched an invasion of

Hispania in 236 BC and became virtual dictator of Carthage before being killed in battle. Father of Hannibal.

HANNIBAL (247–182 BC) Son of Hamilcar. Commander of Carthaginian forces from 221 BC, he took an army, which included war elephants, across the Iberian peninsula, over the Pyrenees and Alps and down into northern Italy in what became known as the Second Punic War. Despite impressive victories he was forced to return home when the Romans attacked Carthage, and was defeated at the Battle of Zama (201 BC) by Scipio Africanus. He then served for many years as chief magistrate of Carthage, introducing all kinds of reforms, before the Romans forced him into exile. Eventually, to avoid falling into Roman hands, he killed himself by poisoning.

HELIOGABALUS (c.203–222) Roman emperor (218–22). Grandson of the aunt of murdered emperor Caracalla, and priest in the cult of the sun deity El Gabal, Heliogabalus was proclaimed the true successor to Caracalla, with some people claiming he was Caracalla's illegitimate son by a union between first cousins. Installed as emperor after the emperor Macrinus had been defeated and executed, he attempted to revolutionize Roman religious traditions and flouted sexual taboos, marrying five times before, aged eighteen, he was murdered and replaced by his cousin Severus Alexander.

HIERO OF SYRACUSE Hiero II, King of Syracuse (270–215 BC). Illegitimate son of a nobleman and one-time general with Pyrrhus, Hiero became commander of Syracusan forces on the departure of Pyrrhus in 275 BC and was elected ruler of the town after defeating the Mamertines (Mamertina was present-day Messina). After fighting and losing a war with Roman forces, he made a pact with Rome in 263 BC, which assured his kingdom's security in return for support for the Romans in their war with Carthage. Hiero was a relative of Archimedes, whose inventions, particularly in the military field, he supported.

JOANNA, QUEEN (1373–1435) Joanna II ruled Naples from 1414 to 1435. Childless herself, she allowed her court to be run by her favourites and lovers, playing off the Anjou and Aragon families by offering prominent members of each succession to her throne. Conflict between the royal lines saw the two most successful mercenary commanders of the period, Francesco Sforza and Braccio da Montone, pitted against each other.

JULIAN Marcus Didius Julianus (c.133–193). Consul under Pertinax, Julian was proclaimed emperor by the Praetorian Guard after they had murdered Pertinax. He reigned for only sixty-six days before he himself was murdered when Septimius Severus, who had refused to recognize his leadership, arrived in Rome.

JULIUS II Giuliano della Rovere (1443–1513), Cardinal of San Pietro ad Vincula, was made pope in 1503 after the twenty-six-day reign of Pius III, who had been elected after the death of Alexander VI. Julius had for many years been a fierce rival of Alexander and was unlikely to be supportive of his son Cesare Borgia. He rapidly dismantled the Borgia family's power and set about ending the feud between the dominant Orsini and Colonna families. Having thus secured his authority in Rome, he reasserted papal territorial rights in the Romagna, attacking the Venetians and taking Perugia and Bologna in 1506. This gave the papacy unprecedented temporal power. In 1508 he formed the League of Cambrai together with France, Spain and the Holy Roman Empire to expel the Venetians from Romagna altogether. But after the Venetians were defeated at Agnadello (or Vailà) in 1509, Julius feared French domination and joined forces with Venice to drive Louis XII out of Italy. Julius was hugely influential as a patron of the arts. He had the foundation stone of St Peter's Basilica laid in 1506 and commissioned Michelangelo to paint the ceiling of the Sistine Chapel.

LEO X Giovanni de' Medici (1475–1521). Made a cardinal at age thirteen, Giovanni, son of Lorenzo de' Medici, was elected pope in 1513, taking the name of Leo X. His papacy was memorable for the sale of indulgences to pay for building work on St Peter's Basilica, his determined promotion of his Medici relations and his response to Martin Luther's ninety-five theses against indulgences. In 1513 he joined forces with the Venetians and various foreign powers to expel the French from Italy, but later allied himself with the French against the Holy Roman Empire.

LOUIS XI (1423–83) King of France (1461–83). Louis increased the power of the king in relation to the barons and added

Burgundy and Anjou to the French throne. In a treaty of 1474 he gained the right to levy troops in Switzerland.

LOUIS XII (1462–1515)   King of France (1498–1515). Louis was the king who got France most determinedly involved in the affairs of Italy. Originally Duke of Orleans, he succeeded his cousin Charles VIII in 1498 and quickly made a deal with Pope Alexander VI that allowed him to renounce his first wife and marry Charles's widow, thus adding Brittany to the French crown. Since the house of Orleans had claims to both Milan and Naples, Louis made an agreement with Venice to split Milan's territory and took the town in 1499. Ludovico Sforza, Duke of Milan, took it back in 1500 but was driven out again. Louis then used the same policy in the south, reaching an agreement with Spain to divide the Kingdom of Naples and taking the town for France in 1501. However, the occupying powers fell out over the terms of the partition and in 1503 the Spanish defeated the French at Garigliano. In 1508 Louis joined the Holy Roman Empire, England, the Papal States, Florence and Spain in the so-called League of Cambrai, an aggressive alliance against the Venetians. Louis led the alliance's army and scored a comprehensive victory over the Venetians at Agnadello (or Vailà) in 1509. But the consequent increase in the power of both Rome and France caused the two powers to fall out and in 1510 Pope Julius II, together with England, Spain, Switzerland and the Holy Roman Empire, formed the Holy League to drive France out of Italy, a goal that was finally achieved at the battle of Novara in 1513. Two years later, however, Louis's successor, Francis I, would return to take Milan and much of northern Italy.

LUCA RAINALDI, BISHOP   An ambassador for the Emperor Maximilian.

LUDOVICO II   Also known as Ludovico il Moro. See SFORZA, LUDOVICO.

MACRINUS   Marcus Opellius Macrinus (c.165–218). Roman emperor (217–18). Macrinus was the first emperor not to have been a senator or a member of a senatorial family. He rose from humble origins to bureaucratic service under Severus and was then appointed prefect by Caracalla and proclaimed emperor after Caracalla was murdered (many believed that Macrinus himself was responsible for the murder). His brief reign was spent entirely in the east, where military setbacks eroded his power-base until eventually he was defeated by supporters of the fourteen-year-old Heliogabalus, grandson of Caracalla's aunt, Julia Maesa.

MANTUA, MARQUIS OF   Francesco Gonzaga (1466–1519). Victorious mercenary commander of the forces of the League of Venice against Charles VIII of France at the battle of Fornovo in 1495.

MARCUS AURELIUS   Marcus Aurelius Antoninus (121–180), Roman emperor (161–180). A Stoic philosopher, his work *Meditations*, written in Greek while campaigning with his army, is still considered a masterpiece. A successful reformer in domestic policy, he faced serious military threats from Parthia and from various tribes in Germany and Gaul. He died of natural causes and was immediately deified.

MAXIMILIAN (1459–1519)   Habsburg ruler of the Holy Roman Empire (1486–1519). Maximilian aimed to unify the empire's heterogeneous possessions by centralizing the administration. He also hoped to recover the empire's dominant position in Italy and to become leader of the Christian world by launching a crusade against Islam. While his domestic reforms enjoyed a certain amount of success, his foreign policies were confused and ineffective and led to the loss of Switzerland, which became an independent confederation in 1499. Although Maximilian hoped to regain territory from Venice, he was constantly thwarted by the need to give precedence to countering French expansionism in the peninsula. In 1495 he joined the League of Venice, which aimed to expel the French from Italy, but gained nothing from participation. In 1496 he was invited by the Duke of Milan (his wife's uncle) to send an army to meet the threat of a French invasion, but France did not attack. Persuaded to move south to help Pisa resist the Florentines, the imperial army surprisingly failed to save the town. In 1507 he began a long-drawn-out attempt to take territory from Venice, but without making significant progress. In 1512 Maximilian joined the Holy League to push the French out of Italy. When Francis I once again took Milan for the French in 1515, Maximilian became involved in yet another, this time unsuccessful, attempt to keep France north of the Alps. Maximilian was succeeded by his grandson Charles V, who became King of Spain as well.

MAXIMINUS   Gaius   Julius   Verus   Maximinus   (c.173–238), Roman emperor (235–238). Born in Thrace and from a humble background, Maximinus rose to become a seasoned military commander and led an army rebellion against the young emperor Alexander Severus, who was abandoned by his own troops and murdered. Hated by the aristocratic Senate, Maximinus faced numerous rebellions and conspiracies, which he ruthlessly suppressed, until he was eventually murdered by his own troops.

MOSES   Old Testament Hebrew leader who led the Jews out of their captivity in Egypt to 'the promised land'.

NABIS   Ruler of Sparta (207–192 BC), ruthless in his determination to return Sparta to its former glory. After a period of successful territorial expansionism, Nabis was attacked by the Romans in alliance with his other enemies. Decisively beaten by Philopoemen, he nevertheless managed to hold on to the city of Sparta before being murdered by a group of Aetolians who were supposedly coming to his aid.

NIGER, GAIUS PESCENNIUS (c.140–194)   Roman governor of Syria, who proclaimed himself emperor after the murder of Pertinax in 193, and was defeated and killed by the forces of Septimius Severus in 194.

OLIVEROTTO   Oliverotto Euffreducci (c.1475–1502). Mercenary commander who took power in Fermo in 1502 and used ruthless force to eliminate his enemies. Oliverotto was killed by Borgia at Senigallia in 1502.

ORCO, REMIRRO DE   Ramiro de Lorqua (c.1452–1502). Military commander in the service of Cesare Borgia. After being involved in many military campaigns on Borgia's behalf, he was given the governorship of the Romagna in 1501. Arrested on corruption charges, he was beheaded in 1502.

ORSINI   One of the two powerful Roman families (the other was the Colonna) whose feuding dominated political life in Rome from the second half of the thirteenth century to the end of the fifteenth. Both families had mercenary armies. Cesare Borgia used the Orsini army in his early campaigns but broke with them when he suspected them of conspiring against him. He later invited the

Orsini leaders to Senigallia with the pretence of negotiating an agreement and had them killed.

NICCOLÒ ORSINI Count of Pitigliano (1442–1510). Mercenary commander who led Venetian forces in their war against the League of Cambrai, and joint commander with his cousin Bartolomeo d'Alviano at the battle of Agnadello (or Vailà) at which, largely thanks to disagreements between the two, the Venetians were routed.

PAULO, SIGNOR Paulo Orsini was leader of the Orsini faction during the period of Cesare Borgia's rise to power. He accepted the invitation to negotiate at Senigallia, where Borgia had him strangled on arrival.

PERTINAX Publius Helvius Pertinax (126–193) was Roman emperor for three months in 193. Proclaimed emperor after the assassination of Commodus, Pertinax failed to give the army the financial rewards they expected, while his attempts to impose discipline antagonized them. He was murdered when 300 mutinous soldiers of the Praetorian Guard stormed his palace.

PETRARCH Francesco Petrarca (1304–74). Scholar, poet and early Humanist whose work on the sonnet form was to be hugely influential in European poetry for centuries to come. The lines Machiavelli quotes at the conclusion of *The Prince* are taken from poem XVI of *Il canzoniere*, in which Petrarch appeals to Italian leaders to stop using foreign mercenaries to fight Italian civil wars.

PETRUCCI, PANDOLFO (1452–1512) A powerful figure in Siena from 1487 when the faction he belonged to toppled its opponents in a coup. From 1502 he became ruler of the town, though always officially maintaining republican institutions. In his role as ambassador of Florence, Machiavelli negotiated with him on several occasions.

PHILIP OF MACEDONIA Machiavelli actually refers to two Philips.

(1) Philip II (382–336 BC) King of Macedonia (359–336 BC), father of Alexander the Great. Coming to power after the death of his older brothers, Philip II rebuilt the Kingdom of Macedonia with a series of wars and astute treaties. He was murdered by one of his bodyguards.

(2) Philip V (238–178 BC) King of Macedonia (220–178 BC).

Followed a successful expansionist policy until the Romans, who had finally defeated the Carthaginians, turned their attention to the threat he posed in 200 BC and comprehensively defeated him in 197 BC, confining him within the borders of Macedonia.

PHILOPOEMEN (253–183 BC)   Greek statesman and general who led the Achaean army on numerous occasions.

PITIGLIANO, COUNT OF   See ORSINI NICCOLÒ.

PYRRHUS (318–272 BC)   King of Epirus, Pyrrhus was an extremely successful military commander and a constant threat to the Romans in southern Italy and Sicily, where he also fought the Carthaginians. His costly victory at the Battle of Asculum in 279 BC led to the use of the expression 'Pyrrhic victory'.

ROMULUS   Legendary founder and first king of Rome.

ROUEN, Cardinal of, later Archbishop of   Georges d'Amboise (1460–1510). D'Amboise was already adviser to the Duke of Orleans when the latter acceded to the French throne (1498) as Louis XII. Louis at once made d'Amboise prime minister and persuaded Alexander VI to appoint him as cardinal as part of a more general agreement between the two. D'Amboise encouraged Louis in his Italian adventures and drew on the support of Cesare Borgia in an attempt to have himself elected pope on the death of Borgia's father Alexander VI.

ROVERE, GIULIANO DE   See JULIUS II.

SAN GIORGIO   Cardinal Raffaello Riario of Savona.

SAN SEVERINO, RUBERTO DA   Mercenary commander who led Venetian forces in 1482 and died fighting for Venice in 1487.

SAUL   First king of Israel, chosen by the people about 1025 BC.

SAVONAROLA, GIROLAMO (1452–98)   Born in Ferrara, Savonarola studied philosophy and medicine before taking up a religious vocation in the Dominican Order of friar preachers. He first preached in Florence between 1482 and 1487 but was largely ignored until, on the advice of the Humanist Pico della Mirandola, Lorenzo de' Medici recalled him to Florence to head the influential monastery of San Marco in 1490. He then began a cycle of sermons denouncing corruption in the town and prophesying doom and foreign invasion. When Charles VIII invaded Italy in 1494 and the Medici fled, his preaching appeared to be vindicated and he became head of the Florentine government, leading the city as a theocracy from 1494 to 1498 and encouraging people to burn anything profane (books, paintings) on his so-called Bonfire of the Vanities. His impassioned preaching against every form of corruption in the Church and his insistence on a return to scriptural purity eventually led to his being excommunicated by Alexander VI, and when he lost support in Florence he was arrested, tortured and burned at the stake in the town's central piazza.

SCALI, GIORGIO   One of the leaders of the briefly successful Ciompi (wool-workers) rebellion in Florence in 1378. Involved in an attempt to stop magistrates punishing a friend, he was arrested and beheaded in 1382.

SCIPIO   Publius Cornelius Scipio Africanus (c.234–183 BC). A Roman general and statesman best known for his defeat of Hannibal at the Battle of Zama in 201 BC. This decisive victory won him the name Africanus. Accused in the Senate of accepting bribes from enemies, he retired from Rome to his home on the coast of Campania.

SEVERUS, LUCIUS SEPTIMIUS (146–211)   Roman emperor (193–211), notorious for his militarization of Roman bureaucracy and the empire in general. After holding military commands under emperors Marcus Aurelius and Commodus, on the murder of the emperor Pertinax in 193 he led his legions to Rome and seized power. In 194 he defeated Pescennius Niger, who had proclaimed himself emperor in the east, and in 196 he defeated another would-be emperor, Clodius Albinus, in Gaul. In the last years of his life he engaged in a long military campaign in Britain, dying in York in 211.

SFORZA, CARDINAL   Ascanio Sforza (1455–1505). Fifth child of Francesco Sforza, Duke of Milan, and younger brother of Galeazzo and Ludovico who each in turn became duke. Appointed as cardinal in 1484, Ascanio made several fruitless attempts to be elected pope. Acting as a spy for Milan in Rome, he was demoted by Alexander VI when Milan aided the French invasion of 1494. Ascanio was subsequently reinstated but lost his power-base when the French took Milan under Louis XII. He was imprisoned by the French for three years before Georges d'Amboise, Archbishop of Rouen and adviser to Louis, persuaded the king to release him in the hope that Ascanio would support his, Rouen's, candidature for the papacy.

SFORZA, CATERINA See FORLÍ, COUNTESS OF.

SFORZA, FRANCESCO (1401–66)   The most successful mercenary commander of his century, Francesco frequently fought for Filippo Visconti, Duke of Milan (1412–47). Visconti had no sons and only one daughter, Bianca Maria, whom he offered in marriage to Sforza to keep the powerful commander on Milan's side, frequently delaying the wedding so as to retain his bargaining power. Having eventually married Bianca Maria in 1441, Sforza expected to become duke on Visconti's death in 1447, but the people of Milan declared a republic. Sforza at first served the republic in a war against Venice, but then betrayed it and took Milan for himself, becoming duke in 1450.

SFORZA, GIACOMO   Giacomo (Muzio) Attendolo (1369–1424). Father of Francesco Sforza, who would become Duke of Milan. Joined the mercenary army of Alberigo da Barbiano in the 1380s and received the nickname Sforza for his strength and determination. Sforza served as mercenary commander for many Italian leaders and frequently found himself opposed to Braccio da Montone, who had also started his mercenary career under Alberigo da Barbiano. He was eventually killed in the service of Joanna of Naples.

SFORZA, LUDOVICO (1452–1508)   Second son of Francesco Sforza, and Duke of Milan (1494–1500). When Ludovico's older brother and duke, Galeazzo Maria, was assassinated in 1476, power officially passed to his seven-year-old son Gian Galeazzo, but Ludovico seized control of the state and eventually became duke when Gian Galeazzo died in 1494. Since Naples favoured Gian Galeazzo's attempt to regain his title, Ludovico supported the claim of Charles VIII to the Neapolitan throne and encouraged his invasion of Italy in 1494. However, the extent of French successes led him to join the League of Venice, an anti-French alliance, which pushed Charles out of Italy. In 1499, Ludovico lost Milan to Charles's successor, Louis XII. He managed to recover the city briefly in 1500 but was then defeated and imprisoned by the French until his death in 1508. He is chiefly remembered for his patronage of Leonardo da Vinci.

SIXTUS Francesco della Rovere (1414–84) was elected pope in 1471, taking the name of Sixtus IV. Sixtus was renowned for his nepotism and in 1478 took part in the Pazzi conspiracy to topple the Medici in Florence. Following the failed assassination attempt on Lorenzo il Magnifico and the execution of the would-be assassins, Sixtus excommunicated Lorenzo, placed Florence under interdiction and, in alliance with Naples, declared war on the town. Sixtus's nephew, Giuliano della Rovere, would become Pope Julius II in 1503.

SODERINI, PIERO (1450–1522) Elected *Gonfaloniere* of Florence and hence head of state for life in 1502, Soderini was a friend of Machiavelli and promoted his career, but Machiavelli found him indecisive and eventually lost respect for him. In line with his predecessor, Savonarola, Soderini maintained an alliance with France throughout his period of government, but he was not an able statesman and had no protection to fall back on once the French were driven out of Italy by the Holy League of papal, Spanish and imperial forces. In 1512 Soderini attempted to resist Spanish forces at Prato, but had to flee the city as the League's forces advanced and a Medici regime was reinstated.

THESEUS Legendary Greek hero, son of Aegeus, King of Athens. He slew the Minotaur in the Cretan labyrinth and was the first lover of the adolescent Helen of Troy. He united the region of Attica under the administration of Athens.

TITUS QUINTIUS Flaminius Titus Quintius (*c.*228–174 BC). A Roman general who led the campaign against Philip V of Macedonia. Titus defeated Philip at the battle of Cynoscephalae in Thessaly in 197. Philip was forced to retreat from all his Greek possessions but his Macedonian kingdom was left intact.

VENAFRO, ANTONIO DA Antonio Giordano (1459–1530). Having helped Pandolfo Petrucci become the ruler of Siena, Antonio was chosen as his first minister and chief adviser and was entrusted with important diplomatic missions to Rome and other courts. In 1502 he was at Magione when Cesare Borgia's mercenaries conspired to betray him. When Petrucci's son, Borghese, lost power in 1516, Antonio returned to his home town of Venafro but later went to serve the government of Naples, where he died.

VISCONTI, Bernabò (1323–85)   Ruled Milan together with two brothers from 1354 to 1385. Imprisoned and killed by his nephew Gian Galeazzo Visconti.

VISCONTI, FILIPPO (1392–1447)   Duke of Milan (1412–47). Filippo was a cruel and paranoid manipulator who rebuilt the Duchy of Milan with the services of mercenary leaders such as Carmagnola and Francesco Sforza. To keep Sforza loyal, he promised him his only child and heir, Bianca Maria, in marriage, then made him wait many years for the wedding.

VITELLI, NICCOLÒ (1414–86)   Military commander in constant battle with papal forces for the control of Città di Castello, a town near Perugia, in Umbria. Forced out of the town by Sixtus IV in 1475, he received support from the Medici after the failed Pazzi conspiracy in which the pope had been involved. On recovering the town, he destroyed the fortresses that Sixtus had built in his absence.

VITELLI, PAULO (1461–99)   Son of Niccolò Vitelli. A mercenary commander who led the Florentine army in its siege of Pisa in 1498. Having breached the walls, Paulo behaved with inexplicable caution, failing to push home his advantage, as a result of which he was suspected of treachery, arrested and executed.

VITELLI, THE   Noble family of mercenary commanders who controlled the town of Città di Castello, near Perugia in Umbria, for most of the fifteenth century.

VITELLOZZO   Vitellozzo Vitelli (c.1458–1502). Son of Niccolò and brother of Paulo, Vitellozzo was serving Florence with Paulo when the latter was arrested and executed for treachery. Vitellozzo escaped and served Cesare Borgia. Together with the Orsini faction, he conspired against Borgia and was among the conspirators killed in Senigallia in 1502.

XENOPHON (431–354 BC)   An Athenian and friend of Socrates, Xenophon was opposed to democracy and spent much of his life in Sparta. He joined a group of 10,000 mercenaries who served Cyrus during his campaign against Artaxerxes in Asia Minor in 401. After Cyrus was killed, Xenophon was one of the generals who led the mercenaries on their 1,000-mile retreat home (fewer than 6,000 survived). He wrote about the campaign in *Anabasis*, one of his many books.

read more

PENGUIN CLASSICS

THE POLITICS
ARISTOTLE

'Man is by nature a political animal'

In *The Politics* Aristotle addresses the questions that lie at the heart of political science. How should society be ordered to ensure the happiness of the individual? Which forms of government are best and how should they be maintained? By analysing a range of city constitutions – oligarchies, democracies and tyrannies – he seeks to establish the strengths and weaknesses of each system to decide which are the most effective, in theory and in practice. A hugely significant work, which has influenced thinkers as diverse as Aquinas and Machiavelli, *The Politics* remains an outstanding commentary on fundamental political issues and concerns, and provides fascinating insights into the workings and attitudes of the Greek city-state.

The introductions by T. A. Sinclair and Trevor J. Saunders discuss the influence of *The Politics* on philosophers, its modern relevance and Aristotle's political beliefs. This edition contains Greek and English glossaries, and a bibliography for further reading.

Translated by T. A. Sinclair
Revised and re-presented by Trevor J. Saunders

PENGUIN CLASSICS

CONVERSATIONS OF SOCRATES
XENOPHON

Socrates' Defence/Memoirs of Socrates/The Estate-Manager/The Dinner-Party

'He seemed to me to be the perfect example of goodness and happiness'

After the execution of Socrates in 399 BC, a number of his followers wrote dialogues featuring him as the protagonist and, in so doing, transformed the great philosopher into a legendary figure. Xenophon's portrait is the only one other than Plato's to survive, and while it offers a very personal interpretation of Socratic thought, it also reveals much about the man and his philosophical views. In 'Socrates' Defence' Xenophon defends his mentor against charges of arrogance made at his trial, while the 'Memoirs of Socrates' also starts with an impassioned plea for the rehabilitation of a wronged reputation. Along with 'The Estate-Manager', a practical economic treatise, and 'The Dinner-Party', a sparkling exploration of love, Xenophon's dialogues offer fascinating insights into the Socratic world and into the intellectual atmosphere and daily life of ancient Greece.

Xenophon's complete Socratic works are translated in this volume. In his introduction, Robin Waterfield illuminates the significance of these four books, showing how perfectly they embody the founding principles of Socratic thought.

Translated by Hugh Tredennick and Robin Waterfield and edited with new material by Robin Waterfield

PENGUIN CLASSICS

THE HISTORY OF THE CHURCH
EUSEBIUS

> 'Could I do better than start from the beginning of the dispensation
> of our Saviour and Lord, Jesus the Christ of God?'

Eusebius's account is the only surviving historical record of the Church during its crucial first 300 years. Bishop Eusebius (*c.* 260–339 AD), a learned scholar who lived most of his life in Caesarea in Palestine, broke new ground in writing the *History* and provided a model for all later ecclesiastical historians. In tracing the history of the Church from the time of Christ to the Great Persecution at the beginning of the fourth century and ending with the conversion of the Emperor Constantine, his aim was to show the purity and continuity of the doctrinal tradition of Christianity and its struggle against persecutors and heretics. He supported his account by extensive quotations from original sources.

This edition of G. A. Williamson's clear, fluid translation is accompanied by an introduction by Andrew Louth discussing the life and works of Eusebius, together with notes, a bibliography, a map of the world of Eusebius and brief biographies of the figures who appear in the work.

Translated by G. A. Williamson
Revised and edited with a new introduction by Andrew Louth

---

read more

PENGUIN CLASSICS

THE DECAMERON
GIOVANNI BOCCACCIO

'Ever since the world began, men have been subject to various tricks of Fortune'

In the summer of 1348, as the Black Death ravages their city, ten young Florentines take refuge in the countryside. They amuse themselves by each telling a story a day for the ten days they are destined to remain there – a hundred stories of love, adventure and surprising twists of fate. Less preoccupied with abstract concepts of morality or religion than earthly values, the tales range from the bawdy Peronella hiding her lover in a tub to Ser Cepperallo, who, despite his unholy effrontery, becomes a Saint. The result is a towering monument of European literature and a masterpiece of imaginative narrative.

This is the second edition of G. H. McWilliam's acclaimed translation of *The Decameron*. In his introduction Professor McWilliam illuminates the worlds of Boccaccio and of his storytellers, showing Boccaccio as a master of vivid and exciting prose fiction.

Translated with a new introduction and notes by G. H. McWilliam

read more

PENGUIN CLASSICS

THE REPUBLIC
PLATO

'We are concerned with the most important of issues, the choice between a good and an evil life'

Plato's *Republic* is widely acknowledged as the cornerstone of Western philosophy. Presented in the form of a dialogue between Socrates and three different interlocutors, it is an inquiry into the notion of a perfect community and the ideal individual within it. During the conversation other questions are raised: what is goodness; what is reality; what is knowledge? *The Republic* also addresses the purpose of education and the roles of both women and men as 'guardians' of the people. With remarkable lucidity and deft use of allegory, Plato arrives at a depiction of a state bound by harmony and ruled by 'philosopher kings'.

Desmond Lee's translation of *The Republic* has come to be regarded as a classic in its own right. The new introduction by Melissa Lane discusses Plato's aims in writing *The Republic*, its major arguments and perspective on politics in ancient Greece, and its significance through the ages and today.

Translated with an introduction by Desmond Lee

He just wanted a decent book to read ...

Not too much to ask, is it? It was in 1935 when Allen Lane, Managing Director of Bodley Head Publishers, stood on a platform at Exeter railway station looking for something good to read on his journey back to London. His choice was limited to popular magazines and poor-quality paperbacks – the same choice faced every day by the vast majority of readers, few of whom could afford hardbacks. Lane's disappointment and subsequent anger at the range of books generally available led him to found a company – and change the world.

'We believed in the existence in this country of a vast reading public for intelligent books at a low price, and staked everything on it'
Sir Allen Lane, 1902–1970, founder of Penguin Books

The quality paperback had arrived – and not just in bookshops. Lane was adamant that his Penguins should appear in chain stores and tobacconists, and should cost no more than a packet of cigarettes.

Reading habits (and cigarette prices) have changed since 1935, but Penguin still believes in publishing the best books for everybody to enjoy. We still believe that good design costs no more than bad design, and we still believe that quality books published passionately and responsibly make the world a better place.

So wherever you see the little bird – whether it's on a piece of prize-winning literary fiction or a celebrity autobiography, political tour de force or historical masterpiece, a serial-killer thriller, reference book, world classic or a piece of pure escapism – you can bet that it represents the very best that the genre has to offer.

Whatever you like to read – trust Penguin.

read more
www.penguin.co.uk